UNDERSTANDING THE HOLY SPIRIT

The Holy Spirit Made Easy

LOLA STRADFORD RICHEY

iUniverse, Inc.
Bloomington

Understanding the Holy Spirit
The Holy Spirit Made Easy

iUniverse books may be ordered through booksellers or by contacting:

iUniverse
1663 Liberty Drive
Bloomington, IN 47403
www.iuniverse.com
1-800-Authors (1-800-288-4677)

ISBN: 978-1-4620-4929-5 (sc)
ISBN: 978-1-4620-4930-1 (hc)
ISBN: 978-1-4620-4931-8 (e)

Library of Congress Control Number: 2011915095

Printed in the United States of America

iUniverse rev. date: 8/18/2011

INTRODUCTION

The very mention of the phrase *Holy Spirit* brings up different thoughts, opinions, and emotions. What, and *who*, is the Holy Spirit?

Having grown up in the church for over thirty years, I have often noticed the various ideas and thoughts people have about the Holy Spirit. As a practicing attorney and Christian, I had a desire to understand the Holy Spirit. I have found the Holy Spirit is often a neglected or misunderstood topic by many professing Christians. Many people think the Holy Spirit is meant for just one denomination of churches.

Therefore, I set out to research and discover the true meaning of the Holy Spirit. I learned the Bible speaks clearly about the Holy Spirit. This book will help bring a clear understanding of the importance the Holy Spirit holds for our everyday lives.

CHAPTER 1
An Introduction to the Holy Spirit

*¹ In the beginning God created the heavens and the earth. ²
The earth was without form, and void; and darkness was
on the face of the deep. And the Spirit of God was hovering
over the face of the waters. Genesis 1:1-2 (NKJV).*

The Holy Spirit is the power of God. He is the active force or the power of God at work in the world and has been active since the dawn of time (Genesis 1:1-3). The Bible establishes that the Holy Spirit is God in the scripture in Acts stating that lying to the Holy Spirit is lying to God (Acts 5:3-4), and through the linking of the Holy Spirit with God the Father and God the Son in benedictions (2 Corinthians 13:14; Revelation 1:4-6) and in the formula of baptism (Matthew 28:19).

God eternally exists in three Persons—God the Father, God the Son (Jesus Christ), and God the Holy Spirit—yet He is one God (Mark 1:9-13).¹ God the Father is fully God, God the Son (Jesus Christ) is fully God, and the Holy Spirit is fully God. During the baptism of Jesus Christ by John the Baptist (Matthew 3:3-17; Mark 1:9-11; and Luke 3:21-22), all three Persons were visibly present together as one as revelation, and witnessed by the people.

---

1 The Holy Scriptures regularly testify that only One God exists (see Deuteronomy 6:4-5; Isaiah 44:6; Mark 12:29-30; 1 Corinthians 8:4; Ephesians 4:6; 1 Timothy 2:5). However, the Holy Scriptures also reveal that God is three Persons in One (Matthew 28:19-20; John 15:26; 1 Corinthians 12:4-13; 2 Corinthians 13:14; Ephesians 2:18; 1 Thessalonians 1:2-5; 1 Peter 1:2; Revelation 1:4).

"The fullness of God" — the Trinity — was fully expressed in Jesus Christ (Colossians 2:9-10).

The Holy Spirit is the only Person of the Trinity currently active on earth. Forty days after Jesus Christ's resurrection, He returned to God the Father (Acts 1:1-10). Jesus Christ is now seated at God's right hand in heaven (Mark 16:19; Colossians 3:1). God the Father and Jesus Christ (God the Son) continue their work on earth through the Holy Spirit.

God the Father, God the Son (Jesus Christ), and God the Holy Spirit are equally and fully eternal—omnipresent, omnipotent, infinitely wise, infinitely holy, and infinitely loving. Thus, the Holy Spirit is the same in substance, power, and glory to God the Father and God the Son (Jesus Christ). These three Agents continuously work together to create, save, and protect humanity on earth (Romans 8; Ephesians 1:3-14; 2 Thessalonians 2:13-14; 1 Peter 1:2). This knowledge should cause us to humbly worship, love, honor, adore, and respect equally God the Father, God the Son, and God the Holy Spirit.

The only difference between God the Father, the Son, and the Holy Spirit are the ways in which these three Agents act as They relate to each other and to the rest of creation. The work of the Holy Spirit is to reveal the active presence of God in the world, especially to the church. He is the member of the Trinity most often *present* to do God's work in the world, especially in the New Covenant age. The Holy Spirit has the role of bringing regeneration or new spiritual life (John 3:5-8), sanctifying (Romans 8:13; 15:16; 1 Peter 1:2), and empowering people for service (Acts 1:8; 1 Corinthians 12:7-11). In general, the work of the Holy Spirit seems to be to bring to completion the work that has been planned by God the Father and begun by God the Son.

The Old Testament did not clarify that the Holy Spirit is a distinct and separate divine person from God the Father. The New Testament resolves this gap. Jesus Christ explained to His disciples that "it is to your advantage that I go away; for if I do not go away, the Helper [Counselor, Friend, Comforter] will not come to you; but if I go, I will send Him to you" (John 16:7). The "Helper" that Jesus Christ speaks of is the Holy Spirit.

The Holy Spirit as bringer of mercy

> [29] the Holy Spirit who brings God's mercy to
> His people. (Hebrews 10:29 (TLB).

So, it has been established that the Holy Spirit is the Person of the Trinity through whom God acts, reveals His will, empowers people, and unveils God's personal presence in the Old and New Testament. The Holy Spirit is absolutely holy in His own nature and the source of holiness in all creatures. His central ministry is witnessing and glorifying Jesus Christ by making known to people who Jesus Christ is (John 16:7-15) and who they are in Jesus Christ (Romans 8:15-17; Galatians 4:6).

The Holy Spirit knows all things

10 The Spirit searches all things, even the deep things of God. 11 For who among men knows the thoughts of a man except the man's spirit within him? In the same way no one knows the thoughts of God except the Spirit of God. 12 We have not received the spirit of the world but the Spirit who is from God, that we may understand what God has freely given us. 1 Corinthians 2:10-12 (NIV).

The Holy Spirit knows all things, even the deep things of God (1 Corinthians 2:10-11). The Holy Spirit's knowledge is equal to the knowledge of God. He knows the things of God as the spirit of a man knows the things of a man. The consciousness of God is the consciousness of the Holy Spirit.

The Holy Spirit is our Guide to the end

14 For this God is our God for ever and ever; He will be our guide even to the end. Psalms 48:14 (NIV).

Moreover, the Holy Spirit guides people in their daily lives and daily decisions as their constant Companion (Psalm 48:14; Acts 10:19-20; Acts 13:2; Acts 16:6). The Holy Spirit is like a road map, as He leads and directs people to all truth (John 16:13). Those who believe in Jesus Christ submit and allow God's Holy Spirit to lead their every daily step (Romans 8:14) because He brings wisdom, understanding, and knowledge (Isaiah 11:2).

The Holy Spirit has been called many names since ancient times. Many of these names appear in the Holy Scriptures, and serve as diverse ways for believers in Jesus Christ to conceive of the Holy Spirit, and to reduce the abstraction in their perceptions of Him.

The Holy Spirit has been called or interpreted as:

- Spirit of God

- Spirit of the Lord
- God's Spirit
- Breath of Life
- Divine Spirit
- Spirit of Holiness
- Resurrection Power
- Friend
- Witness
- Interpreter
- Revealer
- Prosecutor
- Advocate
- Wind
- Motivator
- Empowering Spirit
- Guide
- Comforter
- Encourager
- Restrainer
- Saving Grace
- Sustainer
- Roar of Rushing Waters
- Inspirer
- Helper
- Living Water
- Comforter
- Intercessor
- Strengthener
- Standby
- Christ's Holy Spirit
- Spirit of Grace
- Writer
- Companion
- Counselor
- Peace of God
- Teacher
- Sanctifier
- Paraclete, Paracletos, *or* Parakletos (Greek word)
- Wind
- God's Breath
- Kinship of Spirit

- *Pneuma* (Greek word)
- Seven Spirits
- Spirit of Wisdom
- Spirit of Christ
- God's Presence
- God's Mercy
- Glory of God
- Spirit of Grace and Prayer
- Rushing or Mighty Waters
- Power of God
- God's Power
- Glorious Power
- The Anointing
- Witness for Jesus Christ
- Spirit of Life
- Jesus Christ's Spirit
- Spirit of Sonship
- Spirit of Jesus
- Power of Christ
- The Holy Ghost
- Mighty Power
- Spirit of Truth
- Truth-Giving Spirit
- My Spirit (when God speaks)
- His Spirit (when God is spoken of)

Many respected theologians refer to the Holy Spirit as wind, or as God's breath or power. Spirit is the translation of the Hebrew word *ruach* or *ruakh* and the Greek word *pneuma*, which means "wind," "breath," or "spirit" depending upon the context. In English, the word "inspiration" can mean to inhale and exhale breath, even though this isn't the common meaning (it is used this way in, for example, medicine); "inspiration" can signify that someone is driven to higher levels of awareness or spirituality by the actual act of being filled with someone else's breath.

The wind is a good image for the Holy Spirit because the wind is sent from heaven, cannot be contained or controlled, and can be very powerful (John 3:8). God deployed this Holy Wind of the Spirit to:

- Exercise control over the disorganized waters at the beginning of creation (Genesis 1:2);
- Blow across the earth to recede the flood waters for Noah (Genesis 8:1; see also Psalm 33:6; Job 26:13);
- Bring locusts to Egypt (Exodus 10:13);
- Part the Red Sea to allow the ancient Israelites to pass through and eventually defeat Pharaoh and his army (Exodus 14:21);
- Carry quail over the camp of Israel (Exodus 16:13);
- Transports God on its wings to the outer limits of the earth (Psalm 104:3);
- Dry up the waters (Hosea 13:15); and
- Gather clouds to bring rain (1 Kings 18:45).

A wide range of experiences are attributed to the Holy Spirit. All God's miracles and activities in the lives of people on earth are done by and through the Holy Spirit. However, aspects of the Holy Spirit's works are sometimes credited to God the Father and God the Son (Jesus Christ). God the Father and God the Son manage the Holy Spirit. Prior to Jesus Christ's ascension and return to heaven, many of the Holy Spirit's works and miracles were also performed by Jesus Christ while He was on earth (see John 14–16). Jesus Christ made clear to Nicodemus that no one can control the work of the Holy Spirit because He works in ways no human can predict or understand.

As mentioned earlier, the primary purpose of the Holy Spirit, especially in the new covenant age, is to manifest the active presence of God in the world. When the Holy Spirit is present, this encourages believers and unbelievers to have faith in God, and that God is working to bring blessings to His people.

The works of the Holy Spirit are numerous and include the following:

- Giving and returning life (Genesis 1:1-3; Genesis 2:7; Psalm 104:24-30; Ezekiel 37:1-14; Joel 2:28-32; Romans 8:9-11);
- Empowering people for service to God (Acts 13:2; Acts 20:28);
- Guiding, leading, and directing God's people (Acts 8:29; Acts 9:15; Acts 10:19-20; Acts 11:12; Acts 16:6; 1 Corinthians 2:13; 1 Peter 1:12);
- Inspiring the writing of the Holy Scriptures (2 Timothy 3:16-17; 2 Peter 1:20-21);
- Summoning the memory of (and preserving) Jesus Christ's life, love, and message to tell the world (John 14:26; 1 Corinthians 12:3);

- Authenticating and bearing witness to the power of the Good News of Jesus Christ through signs, wonders, and miracles (Acts 14:3; Hebrews 2:4);
- Teaching the truths of the Holy Scriptures to God's people (Acts 1:16; Hebrews 9:8; Hebrews 10:15-17; 1 Peter 1:11-12);
- Bring glory and honor to Jesus Christ (John 15:26; John 16:14);
- Convincing people of their sins and their need for Jesus Christ (John 16:8);
- Warning people against hardening their hearts towards God's love and guidance (Hebrews 3:7-15, 15);
- Giving spiritual gifts to God's people (1 Corinthians 12:4-11);
- Empowering, energizing, and equipping God's people to share the Good News of Jesus Christ to the world (Acts 1:5-8);
- Bringing the presence of God to believers of Jesus Christ (John 14:16-17);
- Teaching and reminding people of Jesus Christ's message (John 14:26; John 15:26);
- Giving insight, wisdom, understanding, and knowledge of God (Isaiah 11:2; John 16:13);
- Carrying God's blessings and abundance to His people (Isaiah 44:3-5; Isaiah 32:15);
- Proclaiming God's word (Isaiah 34:16);
- Anointing Jesus Christ to pronounce the Good News (Isaiah 61:1-3);
- Giving the inner heart peace, comfort, and rest (Isaiah 63:14; John 14:27; Acts 9:31);
- Calling people to repentance from a life of sin (John 3; John 16:8-11; Acts 7:51);
- Revealing the standard of God's holiness and righteousness (John 16:8-11);
- Bringing God's grace and mercy into the world (Hebrews 10:29);
- Imparting Jesus Christ's truth (John 14:17; John 15:26; John 16:13; 1 John 5:7);
- Pouring God's love in our hearts (Romans 15:30; Colossians 1:8);
- Manifesting the presence and an atmosphere of love (Romans 5:5);
- Giving wisdom (Deuteronomy 34:9; Isaiah 11:2);
- Providing freedom (2 Corinthians 3:17);
- Imputing Jesus Christ's righteousness to believers (Romans 14:17);
- Bringing about unity within the Christian community (Ephesians 4:3);
- Giving power and strength for daily living (Acts 1:18; 1 Corinthians 2:4; 2 Timothy 1:7)

- Providing all people—Jews and Gentiles (non-Jews)—full access to God the Father in prayer (Ephesians 2:18);
- Witnessing for Jesus Christ (John 15:26);
- Searching all things, even the deep things of God (1 Corinthians 2:11);
- Interceding and pleading on behalf of believers (Romans 8:26-27);
- Can be grieved (Ephesians 4:30);
- Bearing witness with our spirit that we are children of God (Romans 8:15-16; Galatians 4:5-6);
- Providing a guarantee of our future fellowship with God in heaven (2 Corinthians 1:22; 2 Corinthians 5:5); and
- Working miraculous signs and wonders that strongly attest to the presence of God in the preaching of the Gospel (Hebrews 2:4).

In the chapters to come, the works of the Holy Spirit will be studied and explained so that people can use the Holy Spirit in their everyday lives.

CHAPTER 2

An Overview of the Holy Spirit in the Old Testament

---

¹⁵ When Moses went up on the mountain, the cloud covered it, ¹⁶ and the glory of the LORD settled on Mount Sinai. For six days the cloud covered the mountain, and on the seventh day the LORD called to Moses from within the cloud. ¹⁷ To the Israelites the glory of the LORD looked like a consuming fire on top of the mountain. ¹⁸ Then Moses entered the cloud as he went on up the mountain. And he stayed on the mountain forty days and forty nights. Exodus 24:15-18 (NIV).

The Old Testament had much to say about the Holy Spirit. Often, the Holy Spirit was manifested in the glory of God and through theophanies (or the appearance of God, in the form of the Holy Spirit, to humans). Through the Holy Spirit, in the Old Testament we see the power of God manifest in:

- Creation (Genesis 1:2; Job 26:13; Psalm 33:6; Isaiah 32:15);
- Revelation to the prophets (Isaiah 61:1-6; Micah 3:8);
- Empowerment for service (Exodus 31:1-6; Judges 6:34, 15:14-15; Isaiah 11:2);
- Inward heart renewal (Psalm 51:10-12; Ezekiel 36:25-27); and
- Protection from enemies (Isaiah 63:11-12; Ezekiel 11:13).

Throughout the Old Testament, the Holy Spirit came to people when they were called by God for a special task or assignment. The Holy Spirit commonly empowered and equipped people with extraordinary strength or abilities in order to be called by God for service. Sometimes, the Holy Spirit came upon people mightily, altering their normal behavior or increasing their strength or other capacities. At times in the Old Testament, the Holy Spirit even came upon non-believers to enable them to do unusual and extraordinary work (Numbers 24; 2 Chronicles 36:22-23).

The Old Testament has many examples of people empowered with God's Holy Spirit. For instance, Joseph had the Spirit of God as God's Spirit within him was obvious and seen to those around him (Genesis 41:37-38). God empowered Moses with the wisdom needed for his life-and-death task: watching over the children of Israel during the exodus from Egypt and their subsequent wanderings in the wilderness (Numbers 11:17, 26). God gifted Bezaleel with wisdom, understanding, and artistic skills for the construction of the Tabernacle (Exodus 31:2-4; 35:31-34). The Holy Spirit empowered Joshua with leadership skills and wisdom to lead the nation of Israel into the Promised Land (Numbers 27:18; Deuteronomy 34:9). During the period of the Judges, the Spirit of the Lord came to individuals and empowered them with extraordinary strength to accomplish specific tasks from God (Othniel in Judges 3:10, Gideon in Judges 6:34, Jephthah in Judges 11:29, and Samson in Judges 13:25; 14:6-19; 15:14). When the Prophet Samuel anointed Saul, the Spirit of the Lord came upon him, resulting in Saul prophesying and changing into Paul (1 Samuel 10:6; 1 Samuel 11:6). Moreover, the Holy Spirit came upon David when the Prophet Samuel anointed him to carry out the job of King to which God called him as King of Israel "the Spirit of the Lord came mightily upon David from that day forward" (1 Samuel 16:13, see also 2 Samuel 23:2). Furthermore, the Holy Spirit came upon Jeshua and Zerubbabel in the rebuilding of the Jerusalem Temple after the exile (Zechariah 4:6; see also Haggai 2:4-5). The Spirit came upon Cyrus, king of Persia, to allow the exiles to return to Judah, when Cyrus received the Word to build the temple of Jerusalem there (2 Chronicles 36:22-23).

The Holy Spirit and a new covenant

> [1] Out of the stump of David's family will grow a Shoot— yes, a new Branch bearing fruit from the old root. [2] And the Spirit of the Lord will rest on Him— the Spirit of wisdom and understanding, the Spirit of counsel and might, the Spirit of knowledge and the fear of the Lord. [3] He will delight in obeying the Lord.
> Isaiah 11:1-2 (NLT).

Several Old Testament prophecies anticipated a time when the Holy Spirit would come in greater fullness and power, and God would make a new covenant with His people (Ezekiel 36:26-27; Ezekiel 37:14; Ezekiel 39:29; Joel 2:28-29). The Prophet Isaiah spoke of One who would come from the line of Jesse and One on whom the Spirit of the Lord would rest. This Person would have the Spirit of wisdom, understanding, counsel, power, knowledge, and the fear of the Lord (Isaiah 11:1-3, see also Isaiah 4:4; Isaiah 32:14-15; Isaiah 44:3-4). This One, called the Messiah, would be the Agent of final salvation and of God's power, and would usher in a new covenant (see Isaiah 11:1-2; Isaiah 42:1, Isaiah 61:1-3).

Elsewhere, the Old Testament prophets predicted the Spirit of God would give God's people an inward cleansing of the heart with an "undivided heart" and singleness of purpose toward Him. No longer would God's people seek many gods, but they would seek and love God only and wholeheartedly because God's Holy Spirit would turn their hard, deaf, immovable hearts of stone into responsive, obedient hearts of flesh, ready to serve the Lord (see Jeremiah 32:39; Ezekiel 18:31; Ezekiel 36:26-27). Furthermore, the prophets foretold the renewal and rebirth of God's people through the Spirit of God, with a final cleansing that would place within their hearts through God's Holy Spirit (Ezekiel 11:19; Ezekiel 18:31). The details of this rebirth were quite specific. God would sprinkle His people with clean (or *living*) water, washing away their old sins and impurities and giving them a fresh start. Israel's hurtful spirit of rebellion would be replaced with a Spirit of obedience for God. The Spirit of God would create a new life and light out of darkness and chaos (cp. Genesis 1:2), producing an entirely new ability to follow God's decrees and commandments with a new heart and a new spirit (Ezekiel 11:19; Ezekiel 18:31).

God promises an outpouring of His life elsewhere in the Scriptures, through which the Holy Spirit would be provided to all people through their faith (see Ezekiel 39:29; Joel 2:28-29; Zechariah 12:10). The early Christian church believed this spiritual outpouring was fulfilled at Pentecost, when God's Holy Spirit came to live in all believers (Acts 2:1-18). This signaled a shift between the manner in which God empowers individuals, a shift that can be clearly outlined when comparing passages in the Old Testament and the New Testament. In the past, the Spirit of God empowered God's people for specific tasks of service for the Lord (e.g., see Judges 3:10; 1 Samuel 16:13). Conversely, the Old Testament prophets predicted that in the future God would give His people more widespread empowerment through God's spirit. The Old Testament prophets predicted the presence of the Holy Spirit would bring abundant blessings from God (Isaiah 32:14-18). This outpouring of

God's Spirit would enable His people to lead holy lives that would constitute a new and immediate relationship with God (see Jeremiah 31:31-34; Ezekiel 36:26-27; Joel 2:28-29). The full extent of these new blessings can be seen in the selection of Scriptures provided here.

Scriptures related to the outpouring of God's spirit, and the development of a new and immediate relationship with God

14 The palace will be empty; people will leave the noisy city. Strong cities and towers will be empty. Wild donkeys will love to live there, and sheep will go there to eat. 15 This will continue until God pours His Spirit from above upon us. Then the desert will be like a fertile field and the fertile field like a forest. 16 Justice will be found even in the desert, and fairness will be found in the fertile fields. 17 That fairness will bring peace, and it will bring calm and safety forever. 18 My people will live in peaceful places and in safe homes and in calm places of rest. Isaiah 32:14-18 (NCV).

3 For I will pour water on the thirsty ground and send streams coursing through the parched earth. I will pour my Spirit into your descendants and my blessing on your children. Isaiah 44:3 (MSG).

31 "The day is coming," says the Lord, "when I will make a New Covenant with the people of Israel and Judah. 32 This covenant will not be like the one I made with their ancestors when I took them by the hand and brought them out of the land of Egypt. They broke that covenant, though I loved them as a husband loves his wife," says the Lord. 33 "But this is the New Covenant I will make with the people of Israel on that day," says the Lord. "I will put My instructions deep within them, and I will write them on their hearts. I will be their God, and they will be My people. 34 And they will not need to teach their neighbors, nor will they need to teach their relatives, saying, 'You should know the Lord.' For everyone, from the least to the greatest, will know Me already," says the Lord. "And I will forgive their wickedness, and I will never again remember their sins." Jeremiah 31:31-34 (NLT).

38 "They shall be My people, and I will be their God; 39 and I will give them one heart and one way, that they may fear Me always, for their own good and for the good of their children after them. 40 I will make an everlasting covenant with them that I will not turn away from them, to do them good; and I will put the fear of Me in their hearts so that they will not turn away from Me." Jeremiah 32:38-40 (NASB).

[18] *"When the people return to their homeland, they will remove every trace of their vile images and detestable idols. [19] And I will give them singleness of heart and put a new spirit within them. I will take away their stony, stubborn heart and give them a tender, responsive heart, [20] so they will obey my decrees and regulations. Then they will truly be my people, and I will be their God." Ezekiel 11:18-20 (NLT).*

[25] *"Then I will sprinkle clean water on you, and you will be clean. Your filth will be washed away, and you will no longer worship idols. [26] And I will give you a new heart, and I will put a new spirit in you. I will take out your stony, stubborn heart and give you a tender, responsive heart. [27] And I will put My Spirit in you so that you will follow my decrees and be careful to obey my regulations." Ezekiel 36:25-27 (NLT).*

[14] *"I will put my Spirit in you, and you will live again and return home to your own land. Then you will know that I, the Lord, have spoken, and I have done what I said. Yes, the Lord has spoken!" Ezekiel 37:14 (NLT).*

[29] *"And I will never again turn my face from them, for I will pour out my Spirit upon the people of Israel. I, the Sovereign Lord, have spoken!" Ezekiel 39:29 (NLT).*

[28] *"And it shall come to pass afterward That I will pour out My Spirit on all flesh; Your sons and your daughters shall prophesy, Your old men shall dream dreams, Your young men shall see visions. [29] And also on My menservants and on My maidservants I will pour out My Spirit in those days." Joel 2:28-29 (NKJV).*

CHAPTER 3

An Overview of the Holy Spirit in the New Testament

⁴⁹ "And now I will send the Holy Spirit, just as My Father promised. But stay here in the city until the Holy Spirit comes and fills you with power from heaven." Luke 24:49 (NLT).

All of the New Testament writers witnessed the active presence of the Holy Spirit during the days of the early church. The Apostle John, who wrote the Gospel of John, 1 John, 2 John, 3 John, and the Book of Revelation, frequently discusses the works and power of the Holy Spirit. Moreover, the Gospel of Luke and the Book of Acts, both written by Luke, have more references to the Holy Spirit than are present in any other New Testament books. Luke emphasized the Holy Spirit's work in developing and directing the early Christian church.

To correctly understand the New Testament's teachings on the Holy Spirit, one must also recognize its connection with the Old Testament. The New Testament is a continuation of the Old Testament message of God's love for the world and His people. On the other hand, the Christian faith is not simply fulfilled Judaism. The New Testament primarily emphasizes the Person and work of Jesus Christ and the work of the Holy Spirit that follows from His life on earth.

Before the arrival of Jesus Christ, God sent John the Baptist "filled with the Holy Ghost, even from his mother's womb" to prepare the people for

Jesus Christ (Luke 1:15). John the Baptist was the last of the Old Testament prophets after more than four hundred years of God's silence (Malachi 4:5-6). Prior to John the Baptist and Jesus Christ, many people believed that the Spirit of prophecy had departed from Israel with the last of the Old Testament prophets. Nonetheless, the Old Testament prophets had predicted God's future salvation through a Messiah and His outpouring of the Holy Spirit into all people (Isaiah 32:15; Ezekiel 36:26-27; Joel 2:28-32). These Old Testament prophecies were fulfilled in Jesus Christ and the eventual work of the Holy Spirit. Jesus Christ declared He was One anointed by the Holy Spirit as the Agent of God's salvation as predicted in the Old Testament (Isaiah 61:1-2; Luke 4:17-19).

> *[17] The scroll of Isaiah the Prophet was handed to Him [Jesus Christ]. He [Jesus Christ] unrolled the scroll and found the place where this was written: [18] "The Spirit of the Lord is upon Me, for He [God the Father] has anointed Me to bring Good News to the poor. He has sent Me to proclaim that captives will be released, that the blind will see, that the oppressed will be set free, [19] and that the time of the Lord's favor has come." Luke 4:17-19 (NLT).*

The Gospel writers, especially Luke, emphasized the Holy Spirit's role in Jesus Christ's life and ministry:

Birth

Jesus Christ's birth authenticates Him as the Son of God. The miraculous power of God's Holy Spirit allowed his conception in the womb of a young virgin girl. Although Jesus Christ was fully human with a body of flesh, He did not inherit the sinful nature of Adam and Eve because of His supernatural conception by the Holy Spirit. Through the work of the Holy Spirit inside the womb of Jesus Christ's mother, the human and the divine were combined in a unique way.

> *[18] This is how Jesus the Messiah was born. His mother, Mary, was engaged to be married to Joseph. But before the marriage took place, while she was still a virgin, she became pregnant through the power of the Holy Spirit. Matthew 1:18 (NLT). See also Luke 1:35, 41, 67; Luke 2:25-27.*

Baptism

A defining moment in biblical history occurred at Jesus Christ's baptism. At

His baptism, Jesus Christ was anointed by the Holy Spirit and given power to accomplish His role as the Messiah (Matthew 3:16; Luke 3:22; John 1:32-33). Then, the Holy Spirit led Jesus Christ into the wilderness where He was tempted by evil before starting His overwhelmingly successful public ministry to the world (Matthew 4:1-11; Luke 4:1-13). Through the power of Holy Spirit, Jesus Christ was enabled to heal diseases, perform miracles, and cast out demons (Matthews 12:22-28).

> [9] One day Jesus came from Nazareth in Galilee, and John baptized Him in the Jordan River. [10] As Jesus came up out of the water, he [John the Baptist] saw the heavens splitting apart and the Holy Spirit descending on Him [Jesus Christ] like a dove. [11] And a voice from heaven said, "You are My dearly loved Son, and you bring Me [God the Father] great joy." Mark 1:9-11 (NLT).

> [38] "You know of Jesus of Nazareth, how God anointed [or gave] Him with the Holy Spirit and with power, and how He went about doing good and healing all who were oppressed by the devil, for God was with Him." Acts 10:38 (NASB).

Ministry

Jesus Christ was clearly the Spirit-inspired leader as He had no "official" authority given directly from the people, but authority given only from God.

> [1] There shall come forth a Shoot [Rod] from the stump of Jesse, and a Branch shall grow out of his roots. [2] And the Spirit of the LORD shall rest upon Him, the Spirit of wisdom and understanding, the Spirit of counsel and might, the Spirit of knowledge and the fear of the LORD. Isaiah 11:1-2 (RSV).

> [17] This was to fulfill what was spoken through the Prophet Isaiah: [18] "Here is My Servant [Jesus Christ] whom I have chosen, the One [Jesus Christ] I love, in whom I delight; I will put My Spirit on Him, and He will proclaim justice to the nations. [19] He will not quarrel or cry out; no one will hear His voice in the streets. [20] A bruised reed He will not break, and a smoldering wick He will not snuff out, till He leads justice to victory. [21] In His name the nations will put their hope." Matthew 12:17-21 (NIV).

> [34] For He [Jesus Christ] is sent by God. He speaks God's words, for God gives Him the Spirit without limit. John 3:34 (NLT).

In the New Testament Gospels, Jesus Christ manifested the active presence of God among the people. In the person of Jesus Christ, God and His Holy Spirit physically entered our world and fully resided in Jesus Christ. Jesus Christ embodied all three aspects of the Trinity: God the Father, God the Son, and God the Holy Spirit (Colossians 1:19; Colossians 2:9).

> *¹⁹ For God in all His fullness was pleased to live in Christ. Colossians 1:19 (NLT).*

> *⁹ For in Him dwells all the fullness of the Godhead bodily. Colossians 2:9 (NKJV).*

Many Christians think of the Holy Spirit as the Spirit of Jesus Christ or the Spirit of Christ (see Acts 16:7; Romans 8:9; Galatians 4:6; Philippians 1:19; 1 Peter 1:11; see also John 7:38; John 15:26; John 16:7; John 19:30; Revelation 3:1; Revelation 5:6). The Holy Spirit in a real sense is Jesus Christ's mode of existence on earth (Romans 1:4; 1 Corinthians 15:45; 1 Timothy 3:16; 1 Peter 3:18). To experience the Holy Spirit is to experience Jesus Christ Himself (John 14:16-28; Romans 8:9-10; 1 Corinthians 6:17; 12:4-6; Ephesians 3:16-19; Revelation 2-3). The Holy Spirit bears the character of Jesus Christ and emphasizes Jesus Christ to the world. Any other spiritual experience should be entirely disregarded by Christians.

The Old Testament predicted that God would pour out His Holy Spirit on all people, regardless of gender, age, or social position (see Numbers 11:29; Isaiah 32:15; Jeremiah 31:31-34; Ezekiel 36:26-27; Ezekiel 39:29; Joel 2:28-32). The Day of Pentecost was a fulfillment of Moses' wish that God would put His Spirit on all His people (Numbers 11:29), and on the vision of the valley of dry bones revived by the Holy Spirit in Ezekiel 37.

The Holy Spirit came on Jesus Christ's disciples (or followers) just before His ascension to heaven (John 20:22). The Holy Spirit served as a Comforter and Counselor, continuing to teach and empower Jesus Christ's followers and reminding them of what He had said to them (John 14:25-26). After the ascension and return to heaven of Jesus Christ, the Holy Spirit was a gift poured out to His followers as promised during His earthly ministry (See John 7:37-39; John 14:16, 26; John 15:26; John 16:12-14). Jesus Christ's ascension and return into heaven marks the beginning of the powerful ministry of the Holy Spirit (Luke 24:49). On the Day of Pentecost (Acts 2:1-4), the Holy Spirit became available to all God's people — men, women, slaves, poor, rich, young, old, Jews and Gentiles — who respond to Jesus Christ in faith and repentance. This outpouring of the Holy Spirit was the beginning of Christianity, and proof positive that the new age prophesied (Joel 2:28-29) had now arrived and signaling that "the last days" had arrived (Acts 2:2-4, 17-18).

After the outpouring of the Holy Spirit on the Day of Pentecost, the number of Christians increased to about 3,000 (Acts 2:41), then to about 5,000 (Acts 4:4), and continued to rise (Acts 5:14; Acts 6:1; Acts 9:31; Acts 21:20).

> [1] *When the day of Pentecost came, they were all together in one place.* [2] *Suddenly a sound like the blowing of a violent wind came from heaven and filled the whole house where they were sitting.* [3] *They saw what seemed to be tongues of fire that separated and came to rest on each of them.* [4] *All of them were filled with the Holy Spirit and began to speak in other tongues as the Spirit enabled them.*
> *Acts 2:1-4 (NIV).*

As mentioned earlier, God's Spirit had been given only to select individuals such as Judges (Judges 3:10; 15:14), priests (2 Chronicles 24:20), kings (1 Samuel 10:10), and prophets (Isaiah 61:1) in the Old Testament. Through faith in Jesus Christ, all people can now receive God's Holy Spirit freely and without measure (John 14:18; Acts 2; Galatians 3:28). The Apostle Peter quoted Joel 2:28-32 as being fulfilled on the day of Pentecost (Acts 2:16-21). The future outpouring of God's Holy Spirit will be accompanied by signs and wonders. Blood, fire, and smoke, along with the darkening of the sun and the moon, are indications of God's coming in judgment to those who refuse to acknowledge God's Lordship in faith in Jesus Christ (see Joel 2:30-32; Mark 13:24; Revelation 6:12).

> [30] *And I will cause wonders in the heavens and on the earth— blood and fire and columns of smoke.* [31] *The sun will become dark, and the moon will turn blood red before that great and terrible day of the Lord arrives.* [32] *But everyone who calls on the Name of the Lord will be saved, for some on Mount Zion in Jerusalem will escape, just as the Lord has said. These will be among the survivors whom the Lord has called. Joel 2:30-32 (NLT).*

The Holy Spirit's resources: Distinguishing Christianity from other practices

Another aspect of the Holy Spirit in the New Testament is the clarification that Apostle Paul provides concerning living out of the resources of the Holy Spirit, and how this distinguishes Christians from Jews (and others). This is an important part of an aspect of the New Testament that we will discuss at length later, and that has already been alluded to—namely, the fact that the New Testament (and the arrival of Jesus Christ, God the Son) extended God's covenant to all people, not just to Gentiles. This inclusion of everyone, regardless of ethnicity or previous practice, forms the cornerstone of today's church.

The Apostle Paul is clear that living out of the Holy Spirit's resources and direction is what distinguishes Christianity from Judaism. A person who believes in Jesus Christ "walks by the Spirit," is "led by the Spirit," and "orders his life by the Spirit" (Romans 7:6; 8:3-7, 14; Galatians 5:5, 16-18, 25). The Holy Spirit living within believers fulfills the prophetic hope of the New Covenant (Jeremiah 31:31-34; Ezekiel 36:25-27).

The Holy Scriptures frequently discuss the day-by-day guidance of the Holy Spirit (Romans 8:14; Galatians 5:18) and walking according to the Spirit (Romans 8:4; Galatians 5:16). God's Holy Word (as found in the Bible) and His Spirit provide step-by-step direction for successful living. God's Word and His Spirit are like a compass that guides believers day by day (Psalm 46:1; Psalm 119:133; Galatians 5:16). The Holy Spirit can communicate His guidance in various ways, including audible words, heart peace, or a strong impression of the lack of His presence.

In the New Testament, the Holy Scriptures provide many examples of guidance and direction from the Holy Spirit.

- The Holy Spirit came upon the leaders of the Jerusalem Council (Acts 15:28)
- The Holy Spirit forbade the Apostle Paul to speak the word in Asia and Bithynia on his second missionary journey (Acts 16:6-7)
- The Apostle Paul was "bound in the Spirit" to go to Jerusalem (Acts 20:22-23)
- The Holy Spirit guided the church at Antioch to set apart Barnabas and Saul (Acts 13:2)
- The Holy Spirit established the elders (overseers) of the Ephesian church (Acts 20:28)
- The Holy Spirit provided guidance through the spiritual gifts such as prophecy (1 Corinthians 14:29-39)

- The Holy Spirit led Jesus Christ into the wilderness for His period of temptation (Matthew 4:1; Mark 1:12; Luke 4:1)
- The Holy Spirit guided Philip to "Go up and join this chariot" (Acts 8:29)
- The Spirit of the Lord on several occasions lifted and directed the Prophet Ezekiel and the Apostle John (see Ezekiel 11:1; Ezekiel 37:1; Ezekiel 43:5; Revelation 17:3; Revelation 21:10)

> [16] *But I say, <u>walk by the Spirit</u>, and you will not carry out the <u>desire of the flesh</u>. [17] For the flesh sets its desire against the Spirit, and the Spirit against the flesh; for these are in opposition to one another, so that you may not do the things that you please. [25] If we live by the Spirit, let us also walk by the Spirit. Galatians 5:16-17, 25 (NASB).*

The contrast by the Apostle Paul in Galatians 5:16-26 between "desires of the flesh" and "desires of the Spirit" means that our lives should be responding moment-by-moment to the desires of the Holy Spirit and not the desires of the flesh. Unfortunately, contrary desires and urges often exist, even in very strong believers. Adamic instincts (the "flesh") constantly distract believers from doing God's will, drawing them down paths that lead to sin, destruction, and death (Romans 7:14-25; Galatians 5:16-17; James 1:14-15). Sadly, this conflict and frustration will be with believers as long as they are on earth. However, believers can control and often defeat these sinful urges by being watchful and praying against temptation and through the Holy Spirit's help and strength (Romans 8:13; 1 Corinthians 10:13; Colossians 3:5; Jude 20). If a believer does sin, the Holy Scriptures state we must immediately repent by asking forgiveness of Jesus Christ, and trust Him to forgive.

The Holy Spirit as the manifestation of God today

The Holy Spirit is now the primary manifestation of the presence of God among believers of Jesus Christ. God's Holy Spirit comes to live inside us as a gift based on our faith in Jesus Christ and God's grace (Galatians 3:1-5). Simply put, the Holy Spirit is God's gracious and personal presence for believers of Jesus Christ; He provides assurances of God's blessings as children of God (Romans 8:16).

In talking of the Holy Spirit in terms of experience, we should never overemphasize particular experiences or manifestations, as if Christianity consists of a sequence of mountaintop experiences or spiritual "highs". This is in spite of the fact that, clearly, such a wide range of experiences existed. However, overemphasizing these experiences reduces the awareness of the presence of the Holy Spirit in our day-to-day lives. We cannot wait for the miraculous to believe in God; His Work is all around us, engulfing us in the Holy Spirit and its power.

In Genesis 1:1-3, the Holy Spirit was at work in the beginning of creation. As the Holy Scriptures close, the Holy Spirit and the Bride of Christ (the church or the people of God), issue an invitation for all who are thirsty to come and drink from the water of life (Revelation 22:17).

> [17] *The Spirit and the bride say, "Come." And let the one who hears say, "Come." And let the one who is thirsty come; let the one who wishes take the Water of Life [Jesus Christ] without cost. Revelation 22:17 (NASB).*

CHAPTER 4
The Holy Spirit Gives Life

*⁴ "The Spirit of God has made me, And the breath of
the Almighty gives me life." Job 33:4 (NASB).*

⁶³ Only the Holy Spirit gives eternal life. John 6:63 (TLB).

⁶ The Spirit gives life. 2 Corinthians 3:6 (NLT).

The Holy Spirit gives life (Genesis 2:7; Daniel 5:23). From the very
beginning, the Holy Spirit moved over the waters on earth, giving life
to the heavens and the earth (Job 33:4; Job 34:14-15; Psalm 104:29). All
creatures and other living things depend on God's Holy Spirit for their very
lives, for the air that they breathe, whether they exist on the ground, in the
sky, or in the sea (Genesis 2:7; Job 33:4; Job 34:14-15; Daniel 5:23). The Holy
Spirit is the life-giving Spirit (John 6:63), the power from above, the seed of
divine life that beings about new birth (John 3:3-8; 1 John 3:9), a river of
living water that brings life when one believes in Christ (John 4:10, 14; John
7:37-39). The Holy Spirit is the source of all life (2 Corinthians 3:6), and God
can withdraw that life at any time (see also Romans 9:19-29).

In harmony with the life-giving work of the Holy Spirit is the fact that
the Holy Spirit conceived Jesus Christ in the womb of Mary, His mother
(Matthew 1:18-20; Luke 1:35). When Jesus Christ returns from heaven at
the Second Coming, the Holy Spirit will also bring life by providing new life
(through resurrection) to the bodies of believers: "And if the Spirit of Him
who raised Jesus from the dead is living in you, He who raised Christ from

the dead will also give life to your mortal bodies through His Spirit, who lives in you" (Romans 8:11 (NIV)).

Regeneration through the Holy Spirit

> ¹⁷ *This means that anyone who belongs to Christ has become a new person. The old life is gone; a new life has begun! 2 Corinthians 5:17 (NLT).*

Most important, the Holy Spirit brings new life in Jesus Christ (often called *regeneration* or *rebirth*). Through heart faith and repentance in the Person and work of Jesus Christ, the Holy Spirit moves a person from death and sin to a new life in Jesus Christ (2 Corinthians 5:17; Colossians 3:10). The Holy Spirit washes away darkness and sin and brings new life, renewing mind and heart. Believers are brand-new people on the inside; they are not the same anymore (Romans 12:2).

> ³ *Jesus declared, "I tell you the truth, no one can see the Kingdom of God unless he is born again." John 3:3 (NIV).*

> ⁴ *But—"When God our Savior revealed His kindness and love, ⁵ He saved us, not because of the righteous things we had done, but because of His mercy. He washed away our sins, giving us a new birth and new life through the Holy Spirit. ⁶ He generously poured out the Spirit upon us through Jesus Christ our Savior. ⁷ Because of His grace He declared us righteous and gave us confidence that we will inherit eternal life." Titus 3:4-7 (NLT).*

The Holy Spirit is the driving force behind a person's salvation and new life through Jesus Christ. Conversion, illumination, regeneration, faith, and repentance are all fundamental works of God through His Holy Spirit. God uses human efforts, drawn forth from God's calling and exhortations, to draw people to salvation. Nonetheless, the Holy Spirit is the power that brings people to faith in God through Jesus Christ. Through His Holy Spirit, God draws humankind to Him. The Holy Spirit leads people to receive God's offer of love and salvation through the Person and work of Jesus Christ as Lord and Savior, and to start a new life with Him. God through the Holy Spirit calls people unto Him from a state of sin and death. Only the Holy Spirit gives birth to spiritual life in a person through faith in Jesus Christ (John 3). With faith, the Holy Spirit brings about complete rebirth and renewal in those who believe in Jesus Christ. Through the Holy Spirit, God makes clear to people's minds and hearts the things of God and takes away their heart of stone, giving them instead hearts of flesh that are receptive for the things of God. (See Romans 8:28-30; 1 Corinthians 1:24-31; 2 Thessalonians 2:13-14).

Jesus Christ: the source of living water

> *37 On the last and most important day of the feast Jesus stood up and said in a loud voice, "Let anyone who is thirsty come to Me and drink. 38 If anyone believes in Me, rivers of living water will flow out from that person's heart, as the Scripture says." 39 Jesus was talking about the Holy Spirit. The Spirit had not yet been given, because Jesus had not yet been raised to glory. But later, those who believed in Jesus would receive the Spirit. John 7:37-39 (NCV).*

Jesus Christ's phrase "born of water and the Spirit" (John 3:5) refers back to the Old Testament (Ezekiel 36:25-27). In Ezekiel, the Prophet Ezekiel envisions a future time where God through the Holy Spirit would cleanse a person who believed in Jesus Christ from sins (by water) and bring a "new heart". Sadly, the original sin of Adam and Eve in the Garden of Eden has the potential to render all humankind unresponsive to God. However, Adam and Jesus Christ founded two distinct humanities. The "Adamic" humanity is natural and earthly, and contains sin and death. The other humanity (that which is reborn in Jesus Christ) is spiritual, pure, and life-giving. The eternal life-giving Spirit of Jesus Christ supersedes the Adamic natural life. The Holy Spirit is the birth of a new life *in* Jesus Christ (see Ezekiel 37:9-14; John 20:22; 1 Corinthians 15:45).

The Holy Spirit as the first taste of everlasting life

> *13 And now you Gentiles have also heard the truth, the Good News that God saves you. And when you believed in Christ, He identified you as His own by giving you the Holy Spirit, whom He promised long ago. 14 The Spirit is God's guarantee that He will give us the inheritance He promised and that He has purchased us to be His own people. He did this so we would praise and glorify Him. Ephesians 1:13-14 (NLT).*

> *21 It is God who enables us, along with you, to stand firm for Christ. He has commissioned us, 22 and He has identified us as His own by placing the Holy Spirit in our hearts as the first installment that guarantees everything He has promised us. 2 Corinthians 1:21-22 (NLT).*

The Holy Spirit living within our hearts as believers is like a taste of the eternal life and power that God represents—a "first installment" that ensures more is to come. The Holy Spirit provides an inner witness to assure all sincere believers of Jesus Christ that they are God's children (see Romans 8:16; Ephesians 1:13-14). Moreover, the presence of the Holy Spirit working within our hearts and lives demonstrates the genuineness of our faith in Jesus Christ and proves that we are God's children. See Romans 8:11; Romans 8:23; 1 Corinthians 6:14; 2 Corinthians 4:14; 1 Thessalonians 4:14.

> *13 And He [God] has put His own Holy Spirit into our hearts as a proof to us that we are living with Him and He with us. 1 John 4:13 (TLB).*

When a person accepts Jesus Christ as Lord and Savior, God fills that person with the Holy Spirit. The Holy Spirit gives new life to a true believer, and that person is not the same anymore (Colossians 2:11-15). Believers are not reformed, rehabilitated, or reeducated; they are re-created — new creations or new lives (Colossians 2:6-7). In addition to God's Holy Spirit, believers also become one with the Trinity (John 17:21). Through the power of the Holy Spirit, believers experience a spiritual intimacy with God the Father and God the Son (John 14:20, 23; 1 John 4:13). The Holy Spirit becomes God's presence in believers' lives. Through the Holy Spirit, God begins to work in the lives of believers on earth.

Entering the Kingdom of God

> *5 Jesus replied, "I assure you, no one can enter the Kingdom of God without being born of water and the Spirit. 6 Humans can reproduce only human life, but the Holy Spirit gives birth to spiritual life. 7 So don't be surprised when I say, 'You must be born again.' 8 The wind blows wherever it wants. Just as you can hear the wind but can't tell where it comes from or where it is going, so you can't explain how people are born of the Spirit." John 3:5-8 (NLT).*

Believers are "born of God" when the Holy Spirit lives in them and brings Jesus Christ's new life (Galatians 3:9). Being "born again" is more than a new and fresh start, but rather a rebirth and a receipt of a new family name based on Jesus Christ's death. With this rebirth, God forgives believers and accepts them. Even more, the Holy Spirit gives new believers new minds and hearts, lives in us, and changes believers from the inside out to become like Jesus Christ. Further, the Holy Spirit changes believers' perspectives; their hearts and minds are renewed day by day by God's Holy Spirit (see Romans 12:1-2; Ephesians 4:22-24). As part of God's family, believers must start to think and act differently (see John 3:1-21).

Just as Jesus Christ was born of the Holy Spirit, believers are also born of the Holy Spirit when they accept and trust in Jesus Christ. A believers' old life dies with faith in Jesus Christ, and they rise anew through the Holy Spirit's transforming power (Romans 6:3-14). The Holy Spirit leads a person's heart and mind to become more like those of Jesus Christ (Romans 12:2) and to reflect the fruits of the Holy Spirit (Galatians 5:22-23). Moreover, believers become adopted children of God through faith and trust in Jesus Christ that is built *through the heart* (Galatians 3:26). As adopted children of God, believers share with Jesus all rights to God's resources, rights, and blessings. Moreover, believers can call God *Father*, just as Jesus Christ did (Mark 14:36; cp. Matt 6:9). As children of God, believers are joined to Jesus Christ and receive the Holy Spirit. Simply put, believers become new people in Jesus Christ, with a new Father and new family (Romans 8:14-17; 2 Corinthians 5:17; Galatians 3:26-27; Galatians 4:6-7).

Heart faith and trust in Jesus Christ

> [9] *Those who are God's children do not continue sinning, because the new life from God remains in them. They are not able to go on sinning, because they have become children of God. 1 John 3:9 (NCV).*

With heart faith and trust in Jesus Christ, the Holy Spirit renews and gradually changes a believer into a different person with the likeness of Jesus Christ in his or her heart and mind. As believers humbly walk, abiding with Jesus Christ, the Holy Spirit transforms their old lives, which were full of darkness, into new lives full of light and hope (Ephesians 4:17–5:20). However, this renewing by the Holy Spirit requires believers to humbly and genuinely turn from their old lives to live according to the teachings of (and faith in) God in Jesus Christ. The Apostle Paul (who experienced a similar complete transformation himself) puts it aptly using images of clothing. Paul calls on believers to put off their old, sinful lives, and to engage in new, pure lives directed and guided by the Holy Spirit (Colossians 3). A person with true heart faith in Jesus Christ will not continue to make a practice of sinning. As believers turn to God, God and His Holy Spirit provide the grace, mercy, and power to live a new life full of God's blessings and heart peace. The Holy Spirit brings new desires to enable people to choose God and do good while turning away from their former pattern of sinful living. Simply put, the Holy Spirit directs people and renews their wills so they can perform good deeds and live a life that pleases God.

Faith in Jesus Christ and reception of the Holy Spirit go hand and hand. It is impossible to have one without the other. To accept Jesus Christ through faith means receiving all the privileges of God, include receiving:

- The Holy Spirit and a new life (Galatians 3:2-3);
- Righteousness and the "blessing of Abraham" (Galatians 3);
- Baptism in the Spirit;
- Membership into the body of Jesus Christ (1 Corinthians 12:13);
- Adoption by God as His child (Galatians 4:6-7); and
- The divine seal and guarantee as God's child (2 Corinthians 1:22; Ephesians 1:13-14).

Some of the Scriptures related to the importance of accepting Jesus Christ, and the potential consequences for all humankind of abdicating the need for this acceptance, appear below.

14 If God were to withdraw His Spirit, 15 all life would disappear and mankind would turn again to dust. Job 34:14-15 (TLB).

29 You hide Your face, they are troubled; You take away their breath, they die and return to their dust. 30 You send forth Your Spirit, they are created; And You renew the face of the earth. Psalms 104:29-30 (NKJV).

10 Jesus answered and said to her [the Samaritan woman at the well], "If you knew the gift of God, and who it is who says to you, 'Give Me a drink,' you would have asked Him, and He would have given you living water." 11 She said to Him, "Sir, You have nothing to draw with and the well is deep; where then do You get that living water? 12 You are not greater than our father Jacob, are You, who gave us the well, and drank of it himself and his sons and his cattle?" 13 Jesus answered and said to her, "Everyone who drinks of this water will thirst again; 14 but whoever drinks of the water that I will give him shall never thirst; but the water that I will give him will become in him a well of water springing up to eternal life." John 4:10-14 (NASB).

20 When He had said this, He showed them [disciples] His hands and His side. Then the disciples were glad when they saw the Lord. ²¹ So Jesus said to them again, "Peace to you! As the Father has sent Me, I also send you." ²² And when He had said this, He breathed on them, and said to them, "Receive the Holy Spirit." John 20:20-22 (NKJV).

⁵ God Himself has prepared us for this, and as a guarantee He has given us His Holy Spirit. 2 Corinthians 5:5 (NLT).

*¹ So now, those who are **in** Christ Jesus are not judged guilty... ⁴ Now we do not live following our sinful selves, but we live following the Spirit. ⁵ Those who live following their sinful selves think only about things that their sinful selves want. But those who live following the Spirit are thinking about the things the Spirit wants them to do. ⁶ If people's thinking is controlled by the sinful self, there is death. But if their thinking is controlled by the Spirit, there is life and peace... ⁸ Those people who are ruled by their sinful selves cannot please God. ⁹ But you are not ruled by your sinful selves. You are ruled by the Spirit, if that Spirit of God really lives in you. But the person who does not have the Spirit of Christ does not belong to Christ. ¹⁰ Your body will always be dead because of sin. But if Christ is in you, then the Spirit gives you life, because Christ made you right with God. ¹¹ God raised Jesus from the dead, and if God's Spirit is living in you, He will also give life to your bodies that die. God is the One who raised Christ from the dead, and He will give life through His Spirit that lives in you. Romans 8:1, 4-11 (NCV).*

¹ For we know that when this earthly tent we live in is taken down (that is, when we die and leave this earthly body), we will have a house in heaven, an eternal body made for us by God Himself and not by human hands. ² We grow weary in our present bodies, and we long to put on our heavenly bodies like new clothing. ³ For we will put on heavenly bodies; we will not be spirits without bodies. ⁴ While we live in these earthly bodies, we groan and sigh, but it's not that we want to die and get rid of these bodies that clothe us. Rather, we want to put on our new bodies so that these dying bodies will be swallowed up by life. ⁵ God Himself has prepared us for this, and as a guarantee He has given us his Holy Spirit. 2 Corinthians 5:1-5 (NLT).

CHAPTER 5
Baptism In The Holy Spirit

⁷ John announced: "Someone is coming soon who is greater than I am — so much greater that I'm not even worthy to stoop down like a slave and untie the straps of His sandals. ⁸ I [John the Baptist] baptize you with water, but He [Jesus Christ] will baptize you with the Holy Spirit!" Mark 1:7-8 (NLT).

John the Baptist announced during his ministry that someone was coming who would baptize with the Holy Spirit and with fire (see also Matthew 3:11; Mark 1:7-8; Luke 3:15-16). John the Baptist was the last Old Testament prophet and the predecessor to Jesus Christ. Prior to Jesus Christ's public ministry, John prepared people for Him by announcing the need to repent, turn from sinning, and be baptized as an outside sign of repentance. John the Baptist focused on repentance from sin, the first step.

With the arrival of Jesus Christ, God the Father provided the complete way a person may receive salvation. The complete way to salvation is to:

- Humbly and wholeheartedly repent and turn from sin;
- Turn to God in Jesus Christ; and
- Place your total faith in Jesus Christ's life, crucifixion, and resurrection as a way of complete atonement (or sacrifice) for your sin.

With wholehearted and sincere faith in Jesus Christ comes baptism in the Holy Spirit. *Baptism in the Holy Spirit* is a phrase that New Testament authors use to speak of the coming power of the Holy Spirit. For those who believed in Jesus Christ during the first century, baptism in the Holy Spirit happened at Pentecost. Today, baptism in the Holy Spirit occurs at the beginning of a new believer's life (conversion). Through faith, Jesus Christ baptizes a person with the Holy Spirit (John 1:33), and the believer embarks on a new spiritual life through regeneration (John 3).

The Holy Spirit brought into the lives of believers

> *[11] But you were cleansed; you were made holy; you were made right with God by calling on the Name of the Lord Jesus Christ and by the Spirit of our God.*
> *1 Corinthians 6:11 (NLT).*

God through Jesus Christ brings the Holy Spirit into people's lives in many different ways (e.g., Acts 2:38; Acts 8:12-13, 36-38; Ephesians 4:5). Typically in the New Testament, baptism in the Holy Spirit comes when a person:

1. Confesses all known sins to God;
2. Repents of any remaining sinfulness in his or her life;
3. Calls on and trusts the Name of Jesus Christ as God to forgive his or her sins;
4. Commits every area of his or her life to the Lord's service;
5. Yields himself or herself fully to God in Jesus Christ;
6. Believes that Jesus Christ is going to equip him or her with new gifts for ministry, and create new empowerment for serving the Lord;
7. Prays (or asks Jesus Christ) to baptize him or her in the Holy Spirit.

Such genuine confession, repentance, renewed commitment, and heightened faith and expectation brings positive results. Baptism in the Holy Spirit brings great blessings from God into the lives of believers, and causes believers to significantly grow as Christians in their daily lives (1 Corinthians 12:13). With this baptism in the Holy Spirit, believers receive from God a sincere and deep eagerness to draw closer to Him. Additionally, at this point in the process of ultimate regeneration many believers find that reading the Bible becomes more meaningful. Prayers become real—believers experience the presence of God in their lives, their worship takes on a tenor of great joy, and they often begin to experience spiritual gifts they had not previously known (Ephesians 5:19-20). Often, a new believer experiences growth in sanctification and deeper fellowship with God, even though his or her theological understanding may be imperfect.

Finally, baptism of the Holy Spirit gives believers an inner testimony that assures them that they are God's children (see Romans 8:16; Ephesians 1:13-14). With Christ's Spirit living within believers, they are united with Jesus Christ and can address God as Father, just as Jesus Christ does (Matthew 6:9; Mark 14:36). Other benefits include:

See Acts 22:16; 1 Corinthians 6:11; 1 Corinthians 12:13; Ephesians 1:13-14; Ephesians 5:25-27; Titus 3:5-7).

When believers ask Jesus Christ to fill or baptize them with His Holy Spirit, they can prepare for a life-changing experience. Being filled with the Holy Spirit is not a "one-time deal": rather, it is a continual experience. The Christian life is one that promotes growth in all areas as we progress. For many people, their growth in the Spirit will be gradual, and extend over all the years that they live. Ultimately, the difference between the initial baptism by John the Baptist and baptism by Jesus Christ rests in the coming of the power of the Holy Spirit (John 1:33). John's baptism called for repentance from sin, but Jesus Christ's baptism included the empowerment of the Holy Spirit (Acts 19:5-6) and everything that entails—regeneration of the heart and mind, a lifelong growth process, and ultimate resurrection in which the body is reunited with the perfected spirit in heaven at the Second Coming.

Baptism by water: a condition of discipleship, a sign of faith

Usually in the New Testament age, if a person wants to follow Jesus Christ, one must "repent and be baptized." To repent means to turn away from sin and evil and turn toward Jesus Christ, depending wholeheartedly on Him for forgiveness, mercy, guidance, and purpose. Water baptism identifies a new believer with Jesus Christ and the Christian church. Water baptism signifies a spiritual baptism in which the believer is united with Jesus Christ and the church by the work of the Holy Spirit (see Acts 2:38, 41). However, without a personal heart commitment to Jesus Christ water baptism makes no difference. To be effective, baptism must be attached to an inward heart change leading to an outward attitude change —the work of the Holy Spirit.

Seven passages in the New Testament refer specifically to baptism in the Holy Spirit. In four of these seven passages, John the Baptist speaks of Jesus Christ baptizing people in (or with) the Holy Spirit. These four passages are:

¹¹ "I [John the Baptist] baptize you with water to show that your hearts and lives have changed. But there is One coming after me who is greater than I am, whose sandals I am not good enough to carry. He [Jesus Christ the Messiah] will baptize you with the Holy Spirit and fire." Matthew 3:11 (NCV) .

⁷ John announced: "Someone is coming soon who is greater than I am — so much greater that I'm not even worthy to stoop down like a slave and untie the straps of His sandals. ⁸ I [John the Baptist] baptize you with water, but He [Jesus Christ] will baptize you with the Holy Spirit!" Mark 1:7-8 (NLT).

¹⁵ Now while the people were in a state of expectation and all were wondering in their hearts about John, as to whether he was the Christ, ¹⁶ John answered and said to them all, "As for me, I baptize you with water; but One [Jesus Christ the Messiah] is coming who is mightier than I, and I am not fit to untie the thong of His sandals; He will baptize you with the Holy Spirit and fire." Luke 3:15-16 (NASB).

³² Then John testified, "I saw the Holy Spirit descending like a dove from heaven and resting upon Him. ³³ I didn't know He was the One, but when God sent me to baptize with water, He told me, 'The

One on whom you see the Spirit descend and rest is the One who will baptize with the Holy Spirit.' 34 I saw this happen to Jesus, so I testify that He is the Chosen One of God." John 1:32-34 (NLT).

Two other spiritual baptism passages by Jesus Christ refer directly to Pentecost (Acts 1:5 and Acts 11:15-18). Then, 1 Corinthians 12:12-13 refers to baptism of the Holy Spirit for unity within the body of Christ.

5 John baptized with water, but in just a few days you will be baptized with the Holy Spirit. Acts 1:5 (NLT).

15 When I [Peter] began my speech, the Holy Spirit came on them [Gentiles] just as He came on us at the beginning. 16 Then I remembered the words of the Lord. He said, 'John baptized with water, but you will be baptized with the Holy Spirit.' 17 Since God gave them [Gentiles] the same gift He gave us who believed in the Lord Jesus Christ, how could I stop the work of God? 18 When the Jewish believers heard this, they stopped arguing. They praised God and said, "So God is allowing even those [Gentiles] who are not Jewish to turn to Him and live." Acts 11:15-18 (NCV).

12 The human body has many parts, but the many parts make up one whole body. So it is with the body of Christ. 13 Some of us are Jews, some are Gentiles, some are slaves, and some are free. But we have all been baptized into one body by one Spirit, and we all share the same Spirit. 1 Corinthians 12:12-13 (NLT).

The phrase "He [Jesus Christ] will baptize you with the Holy Spirit and fire," occurs two times in the New Testament (Matthew 3:11 and Luke 3:16). Being baptized with fire is never to be taken literally. "He will baptize you with the Holy Spirit and fire" means Jesus Christ baptizes a person at conversion with the Holy Spirit and brings the person into the Holy Spirit's presence and power (Jon 14:16-17; Acts 11:15-16). The Holy Spirit saturates, immerses, and absorbs a person, bringing new life. Moreover, the Holy Spirit clothes the new believer with Jesus Christ (Galatians 3:27) and brings the person in the presence and being of God. Most importantly, baptism of the Holy Spirit and fire makes a person aware of his or her sinfulness; the person then desires cleansing and purification (John 16:8). The result of this cleansing is life in the truest sense of the word.

The Day of Pentecost

¹ On the day of Pentecost all the believers were meeting together in one place. ² Suddenly, there was a sound from heaven like the roaring of a mighty windstorm, and it filled the house where they were sitting. ³ Then, what looked like flames or tongues of fire appeared and settled on each of them. ⁴ And everyone present was filled with the Holy Spirit and began speaking in other languages, as the Holy Spirit gave them this ability. Acts 2:1-4 (NLT).

The Day of Pentecost was the point of transition between the old covenant work and ministry of the Holy Spirit and the new covenant work and ministry of the Holy Spirit. Under the old covenant, the work of the Holy Spirit was almost completely confined to the nation and people of Israel. The outpouring of the Holy Spirit to cover all of humanity came after Jesus Christ had risen from the dead and ascended into heaven (see John 20:22; Acts 2). After Jesus Christ's resurrection and ascension to heaven, the baptism with the Holy Spirit and with fire was fulfilled at Pentecost (see Joel 2:28-29; Acts 2). At Pentecost, the Holy Spirit came upon believers in the form of tongues of fire.

The Old Testament predicted God would pour His Spirit upon His people (Joel 2:28; Ezekiel 36:28-29; Isaiah 32:15). The people of the Old Testament looked forward to a "new covenant" age when the work and presence of the Holy Spirit would be much more powerful and widespread (Numbers 11:29; Jeremiah 31:31-33; Ezekiel 36:26-27; Joel 2:28-29). Of course, examples abound in the Old Testament in which certain leaders where remarkably gifted by God and empowered by the Holy Spirit—Moses, David, Samson, Daniel, and many of the writing prophets. However, their experiences were not typical of the vast numbers of God's people. Most of God's people during the Old Testament, rather, were saved by faith as they looked forward to the promised Messiah's coming, but did not have the outpouring of the Holy Spirit in the New Covenant power that we experience today.

The Book of Acts reveals the partial fulfillment of this Old Testament prophecy on the Day of Pentecost and on several other occasions (see Acts 2; Acts 10:44; Acts 11:16). The four Gospels and Book of Acts discuss baptism of the Holy Spirit (see Matthew 3:11; Mark 1:8; Luke 3:16; John 1:33; John 7:37-39; Acts 1:5). The New Testament writers as a whole understood that baptism of the Holy Spirit brings an individual into the New Testament age. The Book of Acts aims to highlight the central importance of the Holy Spirit in conversion-initiation that makes one a Christian (Acts 2:38-39; Acts 11:16-17).

> *38 Peter said to them, "Change your hearts and lives
> and be baptized, each one of you, in the name of Jesus
> Christ for the forgiveness of your sins. And you will
> receive the gift of the Holy Spirit." Acts 2:38 (NCV).*

On the day of Pentecost, the Apostle Peter told the people that if they would repent of their sins, turn to God, and be baptized in the Name of Jesus Christ for the forgiveness of sins, they would receive "the gift of the Holy Spirit" (Acts 2:38). In this passage, the Holy Spirit came upon Cornelius and his household as they simply listened to (and believed) the Apostle Peter's message. Moreover, the Holy Spirit came upon the Apostle Paul's audience when they believed the Gospel of Jesus Christ and he simply laid hands on them (Acts 19:1-7).

In Jesus Christ, we first see the new covenant power of the Holy Spirit at work. The Holy Spirit descended on Him as a dove at His baptism (Luke 3:21-22). When Jesus was filled with the Holy Spirit, the result was strength to overcome the temptations of sin and evil in the wilderness (in Luke 4:1). When the temptation was ended, and Jesus "returned in the power of the Spirit into Galilee" (Luke 4:14), the results were miracles of healing, the casting out of demons, and teaching with authority through his sermons and parables. If Jesus Christ had remained on earth, His physical presence would have limited the spread of the Gospel message, as Jesus Christ could physically be only in one place at one time. After Jesus Christ was taken into heaven after His resurrection from the dead, He was spiritually present everywhere through the Holy Spirit, thus empowering His disciples to go and spread the good news.

The disciples of Jesus Christ did not receive the full new covenant empowering for ministry until the Day of Pentecost. Yet, because of their association with Jesus, the disciples also received a foretaste of the post-Pentecostal power of the Holy Spirit when they healed the sick and cast out demons (see Luke 9:1; 10:1, 8, 17-20 and many other verses). After Pentecost, these believers, who had had an old covenant less-powerful experience of the Holy Spirit, received much greater "power" (Acts 1:8), power for living in the Christian life and for carrying out Christian ministry (Acts 1:8; Ephesians 4:8, 11-13). These disciples also received much greater power for victory over sin (2 Corinthians 10:3-4; Ephesians 1:19-21; 6:10-18; 1 John 4:4). Furthermore, this outpouring meant that the Gospel was no longer limited to Jews, but was extended and made available to all races and all nations for an united church dedicated to the glory of God (Ephesians 2:11 - 3:10).

> [26] *For you are all children of God through faith in Christ Jesus.* [27] *And all who have been united with Christ in baptism have put on the character of Christ, like putting on new clothes.* [28] *There is no longer Jew or Gentile, slave or free, male and female. For you are all one in Christ Jesus.* [29] *And now that you belong to Christ, you are the true children of Abraham. You are his heirs, and God's promise to Abraham belongs to you. Galatians 3:26-29 (NLT).*

> [6] *And Jesus Christ was revealed as God's Son by His baptism in water and by shedding His blood on the Cross—not by water only, but by water and blood. And the Spirit, who is Truth, confirms it with His testimony.* [7] *So we have these three witnesses—* [8] *the Spirit, the water, and the blood—and all three agree.*
> *1 John 5:6-8 (NLT).*

> [13] *And God has given us His Spirit as proof that we live in Him and He in us.*
> *1 John 4:13 (NLT).*

> [24] *The people who obey God's commands live in God, and God lives in them. We know that God lives in us because of the Spirit God gave us. 1 John 3:24 (NCV).*

> [16] *For His Holy Spirit speaks to us deep in our hearts and tells us that we really are God's children. Romans 8:16 (TLB).*

> [6] *Since you are God's children, God sent the Spirit of His Son into your hearts, and the Spirit cries out, "Father".* [7] *So now you are not a slave; you are God's child, and God will give you the blessing He promised, because you are His child. Galatians 4:6-7 (NCV).*

> [33] *Jesus was lifted up to heaven and is now at God's right side. The Father has given the Holy Spirit to Jesus as He promised. So Jesus has poured out that Spirit, and this is what you now see and hear. Acts 2:33 (NCV).*

CHAPTER 6
The Holy Spirit Purifies and Sanctifies

*¹⁵ But be holy in all you do, just as God, the One who
called you, is holy. ¹⁶ It is written in the Scriptures:
"You must be holy, because I am holy."
1 Peter 1:15-16 (NCV).*

At the heart of the lifestyle that God demands of His people is the requirement that they be "holy" (see also Leviticus 11:45; Leviticus 19:2; Leviticus 20:7). One of the Holy Spirit's primary functions is to cleanse humans from sin ("sanctify us") and make us holy as God requires. Through faith in the ministry of Jesus Christ, the Holy Spirit cleanses away our sins (or *sanctifies* us) and makes humans holy on the basis of Jesus Christ's atonement on the Cross (2 Thessalonians 2:13; 1 Peter 1:2). Only through the Holy Spirit are humans able to turn from sin and grow in personal holiness (Romans 8:13-16). This cleansing and purifying work of the Holy Spirit is symbolized by the metaphor of fire when John the Baptist says that Jesus Christ will baptize people "with the Holy Spirit and with fire" (Matthew 3:11; Luke 3:16).

*¹¹ You were cleansed; you were made holy; you were
made right with God by calling on the Name of the
Lord Jesus Christ and by the Spirit of our God.
1 Corinthians 6:11 (NLT).*

When a person becomes a believer of Jesus Christ through faith in His life and ministry, the Holy Spirit declares and makes that person holy and righteous (see Romans 1:17; Romans 3:21-26; Titus 3:5-7). The Holy Spirit converts a person from sin with an initial cleansing (or *washing*) that empowers the person to make a decisive break from the patterns of sin that plagued his or her life and heart. Then, the Holy Spirit gives that person a new heart with God's power to live holy. Moreover, in believers God also produces the growth in the holiness of life. The Holy Spring brings forth the "fruits of the Spirit" within a new believer ("love, joy, peace, patience, kindness, goodness, faithfulness, gentleness, self-control," Galatians 5:22-23) that reflect the very character of God. Then, God's Holy Spirit continually changes believers into God's likeness from one degree of glory to another (2 Corinthians 3:18). A believer remains holy through obedient submission to God and through walking alongside the Holy Spirit (Galatians 5:16-18).

> [5] He saved us, not because of righteous things we had done, but because of His mercy. He saved us through the washing of rebirth and renewal by the Holy Spirit. Titus 3:5 (NIV).

God's ultimate goal for humankind is to make us like His Son, Jesus Christ (1 John 3:2). Only the Holy Spirit makes a person more like Jesus Christ (Romans 8:29). Through faith in Jesus Christ, God's Holy Spirit places inside believers the desire to please and honor God through prayer, worship, love, service, and humility. Thus, the Holy Spirit changes the actions and lifestyles of believers by renewing their hearts and mind, shaping them into perfect likenesses of Jesus Christ, God the Son (see Romans 8:13; Romans 12:1-2; 1 Corinthians 6:11, 2 Corinthians 3:18; Ephesians 4:22-24; 1 Thessalonians 5:23; 2 Thessalonians 2:13; Hebrews 13:20-21). Then, He empowers believers to live daily in obedience and in accordance with God's will and purpose (Ezekiel 36:27; Romans 8:1-4; Galatians 5:16, 22-23; 1 John 3:24). That is why the Apostle Peter speaks of the "sanctification of the Spirit" in 1 Peter 1:2, and why the Apostle Paul speaks of the "sanctification by the Spirit" in 2 Thessalonians 2:13. Only the Holy Spirit sanctifies believers (Romans 8:1-14) and produces within them the "fruit of the Spirit" (Galatians 5:22-23).

The lifelong process of becoming more like Jesus Christ

> [7] You used to walk in these ways, in the life you once lived. [8] But now you must rid yourselves of all such things as these: anger, rage, malice, slander, and filthy language from your lips. [9] Do not lie to each other, since you have taken off your old self with its practices [10] and have put on the new self, which is being renewed in knowledge in the image of its Creator. Colossians 3:7-10 (NIV).

Becoming more like Jesus Christ and His holiness is a gradual, lifelong process that is finally complete when we see Jesus Christ face to face (see Romans 8:29; Galatians 4:19; Philippians 3:21; 1 John 3:2). To remain holy means to keep morally straight, and continually turn from sin and evil practices (see 1 Timothy 5:22; James 4:8; 1 Peter 1:22). Believers are to make a personal effort to do what is right and good (as Jesus Christ would). All believers are to rid themselves of the old life and "put on" the new way of living given by faith in Jesus Christ and guided by the Holy Spirit. To "put on the new self" means that our lives and conduct should match and look like Jesus Christ. The more closely we pray, obey and study about God through Jesus Christ, the more we will be like Him and understand. Every believer has a continuing obligation to study and live Jesus Christ and His work. True faith in God and His Son Jesus Christ always reveals itself in loving actions; works of holiness and Christ-like behavior that pleases God. Believers are not perfect after being saved, but are moving in that direction as God's Holy Spirit works in their hearts.

> *¹ And so, dear brothers and sisters, I plead with you to give your bodies to God because of all He has done for you. Let them be a living and holy sacrifice—the kind He will find acceptable. This is truly the way to [spiritually] worship [or serve] Him. Romans 12:1 (NLT).*

> *¹⁶ Do you not know that you are a temple of God and that the Spirit of God dwells in you? ¹⁷ If any man destroys the temple of God, God will destroy him, for the temple of God is holy, and that is what you are. 1 Corinthians 3:16-17 (NASB).*

> *¹⁹ Do you not know that your body is a temple of the Holy Spirit, who is in you, whom you have received from God? You are not your own. 1 Corinthians 6:19 (NIV).*

Once we become believers in Jesus Christ, our bodies belong to God and not to ourselves (1 Corinthians 6:18-20). For believers, the body is the temple of the Holy Spirit (see 1 Corinthians 3:16-17; 1 Corinthians 6:19; Ephesians 2:21-22; 2 Corinthians 6:16; Romans 14:7-9; 2 Corinthians 5:14-15). As believers, God calls us to live as His holy people (1 Corinthians 1:2). When we accept Jesus Christ as Lord and Savior, the God's Holy Spirit fills us and gives us the power to remain holy as we humbly walk in obedience with God (1 Corinthians 6:11; 2 Thessalonians 2:13; 2 Peter 1:3-4). But before believers can live in the newness of life, they must also be dead to sin, and continually confess any new sins as these sins manifest.

As all of us are imperfect, it is inevitable that even one who has been saved will sin, and will need to turn to Jesus Christ. Recognizing this is a vital part of living a life in the Holy Spirit. Every part of a believer's life is to reflect Jesus Christ and the fruits of the Holy Spirit (Romans 12:1-2; Galatians 5:22-23). Believers' lives are to be noticeably different from that of the unholy world around them.

> [2] *He [God] made you holy by means of Christ Jesus,*
> *just as He did for all people everywhere who call on the*
> *Name of our Lord Jesus Christ, their Lord and ours.*
> *1 Corinthians 1:2 (NLT).*

> [18] *But we Christians have no veil over our faces; we can*
> *be mirrors that brightly reflect the glory of the Lord. And*
> *as the Spirit of the Lord works within us, we become*
> *more and more like Him. 2 Corinthians 3:18 (TLB).*

> [20] *I have been crucified with Christ; it is no longer I who*
> *live, but Christ who lives in me; and the life I now live*
> *in the flesh I live by faith in the Son of God, who loved*
> *me and gave Himself for me. Galatians 2:20 (RSV).*

> [13] *You are saved by the Spirit that makes you holy and by*
> *your faith in the truth.* [14] *God used the Good News that we*
> *preached to call you to be saved so you can share in the glory*
> *of our Lord Jesus Christ. 2 Thessalonians 2:13-14 (NCV).*

CHAPTER 7
Sin and the Holy Spirit

2 "Speak to all the congregation of the children of Israel, and say to them: 'You shall be holy, for I the Lord your God am holy.'" Leviticus 19:2 (NKJV).

In all God does, He is holy, perfect, and loving. The essence of God is holiness; God has not evil or sin in Him. Just as God is holy, God wants **ALL** people to be holy (Leviticus 19:1; 1 Peter 1:15-16). People are declared holy when they turn to God through faith in His Son Jesus Christ with heart love, devotion, and obedience to Him. This heart love for God ushers in God's Holy Spirit, which brings peace, joy, and eternal salvation.

Throughout the Old Testament and the New Testament, the Holy Spirit was present when people loved and humbly obeyed God and related in a righteous manner to each other (e.g., see 2 Chronicles 7:14-17; Micah 6:6-8; Psalm 72:7; Isaiah 32:17; Psalm 48:22; Psalm 57:1-2; John 14:27; Galatians 5:22). With this love and obedience, God's Holy Spirit was present as a guarantee of God's blessings and mercy (2 Corinthians 1:22; 2 Corinthians 5:5; Ephesians 1:13-14).

Nonetheless, many examples in both the Old and New Testament reveal that sin and lack of righteousness can withdraw the presence of God's Holy Spirit. Persistent sin, disobedience, or rebellion grieves God's Holy Spirit (See Genesis 6:3, Isaiah 63:10). Sin breaks God's heart, making God our enemy rather than our friend (see Psalm 106:33; Matthew 12:32; Mark 3:29). Most importantly, sin causes God's Holy Spirit to depart and leave (1 Samuel 16:14;

Ezekiel chapters 8 – 11). When God's Holy Spirit departs, God takes away His grace, blessings, and presence (Hebrews 10:29). It is worth mentioning that Jesus Christ was wholly without sin and the Holy Spirit remained within Him, and without limit (John 1:32; John 3:34).

In the Old Testament, the Holy Spirit came mightily upon Samson on several occasions but withdrew when he persisted in sin (e.g. Judges 13:25; Judges 14:6; Judges 16:20). Similarly, God withdrew His Holy Spirit when the people of Israel rebelled and aggrieved the Holy Spirit (Isaiah 63:10). The Holy Spirit departs due to sin, disobedience, hardness of heart, and lack of repentance for sin towards God. A departure of God's Spirit often led to a leaders' failure and torment (see Judges 16:20; 1 Samuel 16:14; Isaiah 63:10). Both Saul and David received the Spirit of God when they were anointed king of Israel (1 Samuel 10:1-10; 1 Samuel 16:13). The Holy Spirit departed from King Saul due his disobedience towards God (1 Samuel 16:14). After King David's sin of adultery with Bathsheba, he earnestly prayed to God for His Spirit not to leave him (Psalm 51:10-12).

> [10] But they rebelled against Him [God] and grieved His Holy Spirit. So He became their enemy and fought against them. Isaiah 63:10 (NLT).

> [3] Then the Lord said, "My Spirit will not put up with humans for such a long time, for they are only mortal flesh. In the future, their normal lifespan will be no more than 120 years." Genesis 6:3 (NLT).

> [14] Now the Spirit of the Lord had left Saul, and the Lord sent a tormenting spirit that filled him with depression and fear. 1 Samuel 16:14 (NLT).

> [11] Do not cast me away from Your presence, And do not take Your Holy Spirit from me. Psalms 51:11 (NKJV).

> [29] the Holy Spirit who brings God's mercy to His people. Hebrews 10:29 (TLB).

God's Holy Spirit for all people: The New Testament age

> [11] You will make known to Me the path of life; In Your presence is fullness of joy; In Your right hand there are pleasures forever. Psalms 16:11 (NASB).

In the present New Testament age, God's Holy Spirit is given to all people who place their faith, trust, and hope in Jesus Christ as Lord and Savior (see Acts 2:14-21; Ephesians 1:13-14; 1 Corinthians 12:1-11). The Holy Spirit gives all people the power to live morally renewed, righteous, and holy lives through faith in Jesus Christ. God's righteousness comes through the surrender of our hearts and lives to God through Jesus Christ and wholeheartedly loving and obeying Him as our God.

> 26 Dear friends, if we deliberately continue sinning after we have received knowledge of the Truth, there is no longer any sacrifice that will cover these sins. 27 There is only the terrible expectation of God's judgment and the raging fire that will consume His enemies. 28 For anyone who refused to obey the law of Moses was put to death without mercy on the testimony of two or three witnesses. 29 Just think how much worse the punishment will be for those who have trampled on the Son of God, and have treated the blood of the covenant, which made us holy, as if it were common and unholy, and have insulted and disdained the Holy Spirit who brings God's mercy to us. Hebrews 10:26-29 (NLT).

The Old Testament departure of the Holy Spirit from Saul also has a New Testament parallel that is found in warnings not to sin against the Holy Spirit and not to bring sorrow to the Holy Spirit (see Mark 3:28-29; Ephesians 4:30; Hebrews 6:1-8). When people deliberately reject Jesus Christ's freely offered salvation through faith, they reject God's most precious gift. In essence, these people grieve and disobey the guidance of God's Holy Spirit, which communicates God's saving love. Today, there is no other acceptable sacrifice for sin other than the death of Jesus Christ on the Cross at Calvary (see Acts 4:12). When anyone deliberately rejects the unselfish and loving sacrifice of Jesus Christ, they are causing grief in the Holy Spirit (Hebrews 6:4-6; 1 John 5:16-21). The knowing, conscious, and willful rejection of the Holy Spirit's witness of Jesus Christ, and the attribution to evil of God's gracious Holy Spirit in Jesus Christ, is called an *unpardonable sin,* both in this world and the next (Matthew 12:31-32; Mark 3:28-29; Luke 12:10). Moreover, the Holy Scriptures make it very clear that God promises to forgive all sins of people if they turn from evil and turn to God *except* in instances where an individual blasphemes the Holy Spirit.

> 28 I tell you the truth, all sins that people do and all the things people say against God can be forgiven. 29 But anyone who speaks against the Holy Spirit will never be forgiven; he is guilty of a sin that continues forever. Mark 3:28-29 (NCV).

A person who *blasphemes the Holy Spirit* attributes the work of God's Holy Spirit to an evil and unclean spirit, and refuses to acknowledge God's power in Jesus Christ. This refusal indicates a deliberate and irreversible hardness of heart. In Mark 3:20-30 and Matthew 12:22-37, the Pharisees and teachers of the religious law assigned the miracles of Jesus Christ to an unclean spirit instead of the Holy Spirit. They in essence rejected the Holy Spirit's work in Jesus Christ and attached the miraculous work of Jesus Christ to an impure and evil spirit. Resisting and judging the work of God led the Pharisees and the teachers of religious law to blaspheme the Holy Spirit.

Believers sometimes worry if they have accidentally committed this unforgivable sin. However, one who truly believes should not need to worry about blasphemy. This sin is a deliberate and intentional attribution of the pure work of the Holy Spirit to the work of evil. With blasphemy, an individual reveals an unrepentant attitude that does not have heart-faith in the Holy Spirit and in the things of God. One who blasphemes the Holy Spirit rejects his leading and his testimony of Jesus Christ; he or she literally rejects God. Therefore, it stands to reason that only people who have turned their backs on God and rejected all faith need worry of this pernicious sin.

> *4 There is no use trying to bring you back to the Lord again if you have once understood the Good News and tasted for yourself the good things of heaven and shared in the Holy Spirit, 5 and know how good the Word of God is, and felt the mighty powers of the world to come, 6 and then have turned against God. You cannot bring yourself to repent again if you have nailed the Son of God to the cross again by rejecting Him, holding Him up to mocking and to public shame. Hebrews 6:4-6 (TLB).*

Another version of the unpardonable sin occurs when a professing believer of Jesus Christ turns away from following Jesus Christ as described in Hebrews 6:4-8, which involves apostasy and is one of the most difficult passages in the New Testament. This passage gives a harsh warning and describes the spiritual death of the person who stops following Jesus Christ, preferring instead to turn back to sin. These people have heard the word of God's love through Jesus Christ preached to them (Hebrews 2:3-4; Hebrews 4:1-2) and experienced God's blessings of the Holy Spirit. Yet, these people turned away from God. This image is suggestive of the wilderness wanderers who turned away from obeying God and fell in the desert (Hebrews 3:17; Hebrews 4:11; Numbers 14:1-4, 29-30). When people turn away from Jesus Christ and His sacrificial death on the Cross at Calvary, it is impossible for them to find any other means of repentance. Rejecting Jesus Christ means rejecting and nailing Him to the Cross once again (see Matt 27:39-44).

> *20 My old self has been crucified with Christ. It is no longer I who live, but Christ lives in me. So I live in this earthly body by trusting in the Son of God, who loved me and gave Himself for me. Galatians 2:20 (NLT).*

As a believer of Jesus Christ, our old life has been crucified with Christ (see Romans 6:5-11). The Holy Spirit frees people from sin that leads to death.

The believer's power over sin and new life comes simply from faith and trust in Jesus Christ's message, life, death, burial, and resurrection (see Romans 6:1-12). Because believers have been crucified with Christ, we have been raised with Him into a new life (Romans 6:5). And in our daily lives, believers have Jesus Christ's resurrection power (the Holy Spirit) to help us defeat sin and evil (Ephesians 1:19-20). Believers, having experienced Jesus Christ's death and resurrection (Romans 6:1-14) through faith, have new hearts and the presence of Christ's Spirit living within (see Jeremiah 31:31-34; 32:38-41; Ezekiel 11:19-20; Ezekiel 36:24-31; Romans 8:9-11; Ephesians 3:16-19; Colossians 1:27; Colossians 3:1-17).

Bringing sorrow (grief) to the Holy Spirit

> *30 And do not bring sorrow to God's Holy Spirit by the way you live. Remember, He has identified you as His own, guaranteeing that you will be saved on the day of redemption. Ephesians 4:30 (NLT).*

The Holy Scriptures encourages people not to "to sin against," "not to resist," and not "to grieve" the Holy Spirit (Isaiah 63:10). *Bringing grief to the Holy Spirit* can be defined as the act of willfully upsetting His leading through disobedience or rebellion. Continuing sin, disobedience, and disbelief towards God grieves the Holy Spirit (See Psalm 106:33; Matthew 12:32; Mark 3:29) and makes God your enemy. The disobedience of God brings severe consequences; this is not a popular theme in the Holy Scriptures, but it appears often enough to be completely clear (see, e.g., Genesis 9:5-6; Numbers 35:16-21; Leviticus 20:10; Zechariah 5:4). The departure of God's Holy Spirit removes the blessings of God from a person or group of people.

Examples of people who aggrieved God's Holy Spirit include the period during which the people of Israel wandered in the wilderness (see the Book of Numbers), the sinful period of disobedience in the Judges (see the Book of Judges), and the period leading up to the Exile (see the Book of Jeremiah). In the Prophet Ezekiel's vision found in Ezekiel chapters 8–11, he sees the outrageous sins that have polluted the Temple in Jerusalem and forced God's glory to depart. God was not removed from the Temple by the Babylonian army. Rather, God departed the Temple because His people were corrupted with sin and thereby drove Him away from the land promised to Abraham, Isaac, and Jacob. Essentially, the Prophet Ezekiel revealed that sin drove God's Holy Spirit away. Without God's glorious presence, the Temple was an empty shell awaiting destruction.

By intentionally turning away from God through Jesus Christ, a person cuts themselves off from God's love, forgiveness, and blessings. Sadly, God brings just consequences to those who turn to sin and away from Him (see e.g. Proverbs 1:24-31; Jeremiah 11:11; Matthew 5:22; Matthew 16:27; Matthew 23:13; Matthew 24:10-13; Matthew 25:41-46; Galatians 1:6-9; 2 Timothy 3:1-9; 2 Peter 2; 1 John 2:18-19). Those who reject Jesus Christ will never be saved. Jesus Christ warned people against hardness of heart that makes repentance impossible for the sinner. Sins that do not involve ultimate apostasy can end in repentance and restoration (see James 5:20). Our resolve to faithfully follow Jesus can be built by taking the consequences of rebellion seriously.

The Holy Scriptures provide us with another way to live that does not involve rebellion and the hardening of our hearts towards God. The Holy Scriptures teach that we should be loving, forgiving, faithful, obedient, and humble towards God, and love others (Micah 6:6-8; Matthew 22:34-40). On the other hand, believers whose conduct is pleasing to God bring the Holy Spirit's presence and God's great blessing (See 2 Chronicles 7:14-17; Micah 6:6-8; Revelation 19:8). All work done for God must be done in the power of the Holy Spirit.

CHAPTER 8

The Holy Spirit is present everywhere

⁷ I can never escape from your Spirit! I can never get away from your presence! ⁸ If I go up to heaven, You are there; if I go down to the grave, You are there. ⁹ If I ride the wings of the morning, if I dwell by the farthest oceans, ¹⁰ even there Your hand will guide me, and Your strength will support me. Psalms 139:7-10 (NLT).

²³ Am I a God who is only in one place and cannot see what they are doing? ²⁴ Can anyone hide from Me? Am I not everywhere in all of heaven and earth? Jeremiah 23:23-24 (TLB).

God is everywhere — present in all the heavens and all the earth through his Holy Spirit (Jeremiah 23:23-24). The presence of the Holy Spirit is the presence of God. As Spirit, God is present with His people everywhere and at all times; He has the capacity to be present everywhere in the world at once. Because God is omnipresent, we can never be lost to His presence through His Holy Spirit. This is Good News because no matter what we do or where we go, we can never be far from God's comforting omnipresence (see Romans 8:35-39).

³⁵ Can anything ever separate us from Christ's love? ... ³⁸ And I am convinced that nothing can ever separate us from God's love. Neither death nor life, neither angels nor demons, neither our fears for today nor our worries about tomorrow—not even the powers of hell can separate us from God's love. ³⁹ No power in the sky above or in the earth below—indeed, nothing in all creation will ever be able to separate us from the love of God that is revealed in Christ Jesus our Lord. Romans 8:35, 38-39 (NLT).

Through the Holy Spirit, God is *immanent,* or present in day-to-day human existence. Because God is omnipresent, He is fully able to give complete attention to each individual at the same time (see also Psalm 139:7-10; Acts 17:24-28). No one is ever lost to God's Holy Spirit. God the Father, God the Son, and God the Holy Spirit are omnipresent together. God's omnipresence makes Him different from any other gods.

> *[23] The time is coming when the true worshipers will worship the Father in spirit and truth, and that time is here already. You see, the Father too is actively seeking such people to worship Him. [24] God is Spirit, and those who worship Him must worship in spirit and truth. John 4:23-24 (NCV).*

Since God is everywhere, He can be worshiped anywhere, any place, and at any time. God cannot be seen by our bodily senses because He has no parts, no size, no space, and no measurement. God is not a physical being made of matter. Moreover, God cannot be limited by material space because He creates space (Genesis 1:1). Most people have a sense of God's presence within the world.

> *[16] And I will ask the Father, and He will give you another Advocate, who will never leave you. [17] He is the Holy Spirit, who leads into all truth. The world cannot receive Him, because it isn't looking for Him and doesn't recognize Him. But you know Him, because He lives with you now and later will be in you. [18] No, I will not abandon you as orphans—I will come to you. John 14:16-18 (NLT).*

God cares about this world He created. He is living and working in this world through His Holy Spirit. A believer can look to the Holy Spirit for all spiritual good as our divine Teacher and Sanctifier. True love and worship of God occurs as God's Holy Spirit reveals God's truth and reality to the worshiper (John 14:6, 17; John 15:26). The Holy Spirit helps believers worship and serve God because the Holy Spirit prays for us (Romans 8:26), teaches us the words of Jesus Christ (John 14:26), and tells us we are loved by God (Romans 5:5).

The presence of God is seen in today's world and the Holy Scriptures. God's presence is revealed with His glory (see Exodus 16:7-10; Isaiah 6:3; Ephesians

1:12-17; Hebrews 1:3). Also, God revealed His presence as Father and Creator, as Jesus Christ and Savior, and as Holy Spirit and Comforter.

Moreover, God revealed His presence in the Holy Scriptures. Moses experienced God's presence on the mountain in the wilderness in Exodus 3. Also, the Prophet Isaiah witnessed God's presence in the Jerusalem Temple in Isaiah 6. The Apostle Paul experienced the presence of God on the highway in Damascus in Acts 9.

The Book of Acts frequently reveals the presence and power of the Holy Spirit. In Acts, the enlargement, development, and growth of the church took place entirely under the power and guidance of the Holy Spirit (e.g., Acts 2:4, Acts 41-47; Acts 4:31; Acts 5:32; Acts 8:15-29; Acts 9:31). Because of the importance of the Holy Spirit's work in the Book of Acts, the Book has often been called "the Acts of the Holy Spirit."

Jesus Christ spoke in John 14 during His earthly ministry of the Holy Spirit's influence on the growth of the Church. The Holy Spirit's presence was clear in the selection of Spirit-filled leaders to care for the needs of the early church's widows (Acts 6:1-7) and in the appointing of Barnabas and Saul for missionary service (Acts 13:1-5). When the first church council gathered to consider the membership of Gentiles into the church, Jesus Christ's first disciples followed the Holy Spirit's direction and guidance (Acts 15:28). Christian workers such as Stephen and Philip were filled with the Holy Spirit's power and proclaimed the Good News by His power (Acts 6 – 8). Moreover, the Apostle Paul's ministry was charged with the Holy Spirit's presence from the beginning (Acts 9:17).

> [11] *You will make known to me the path of life; In Your presence is fullness of joy; In Your right hand there are pleasures forever. Psalms 16:11 (NASB).*

Fulfillment and well-being comes from and completely depends on God's presence. King David, who wrote Psalm 16, found the secret to joy. True joy is far deeper than happiness. Happiness is temporary because it is based on external circumstances, but true joy is based on God's Presence within us through our heart faith in Jesus Christ. (See also Acts 2:28).

God has complete and total access to His entire creation — even "heaven and the highest heaven cannot contain" Him (1 Kings 8:27). Yet, God willingly comes to live in a person's heart through His Holy Spirit for all those who truly love Him. God is present everywhere, but His actions may be different depending on His presence, and on whether those who love Him are acting in accordance with his teachings. Often, God is present to bless His children (Psalm 16:11); at other times, God brings justice and punishes individuals for acts of sin and unrighteousness (Amos 9:1-4).

The Holy Scriptures most often describe the Holy Spirit as being present to do God's work in the world. From the beginning of creation, the Holy Spirit's work is to finish and sustain what God the Father has planned and God the Son (Jesus Christ) has started (Genesis 1:2). In the four Gospels found in the New Testament, Jesus Christ exhibited the Presence of God among the people. At Pentecost, the Holy Spirit came and poured out His power to believers and to the Church (Acts 2:4, 17-18; Acts 10:38). After Jesus Christ's ascension and return to heaven, the Holy Spirit is now the primary expression, sign, and manifestation of the presence of the Trinity.

The Holy Spirit as an Advocate

> [16] "I will ask the Father, and He will give you another Helper, that He may be with you forever; [17] that is the Spirit of Truth, whom the world cannot receive, because it does not see Him or know Him, but you know Him because He abides **with** you and will be **in** you. [18] I will not leave you as orphans; I will come to you." John 14:16-18 (NASB).

Jesus Christ promised believers an Advocate (also called Comforter, Encourager, or Counselor) to be with and within them after He returned to heaven. This Advocate is the Holy Spirit. The Holy Spirit is the presence of God in Jesus Christ Himself abiding with believers (Matthew 28:20). The word, translated as *Counselor* in John 14:16, combines the ideas of comfort and counsel. The Holy Spirit is a powerful Person working for and within believers of Jesus Christ.

When Jesus Christ ascended into heaven, His *physical* presence left the disciples (Acts 1:9). The Holy Spirit is Jesus Christ's Presence, and never leaves true disciples of Jesus Christ then and today (John 14:26; Acts 1:4-5). Jesus Christ is spiritually present everywhere through the Holy Spirit, and living inside each believer (Acts 1:4).

Jesus Christ promised in John 14:18 that believers would never be spiritual orphans and that He would return to them (John 14:1-4). So believers are never alone. The Holy Spirit counsels, loves, protects, comforts, and defends believers of Jesus Christ. Jesus Christ through the Holy Spirit is our constant Companion and Guide as we make our way through life. He guides and directs believers through His Holy Spirit and even gives believers words to say (Matthew 10:19-20).

Jesus Christ on four occasions used the Greek word *paraklētos* to describe the Holy Spirit. The Greek word *paraklētos* means "called alongside" or "to advocate" (John 14:16, 26; John 15:26; John 16:7). The background of the Greek term refers to a legal advocate in the law court where the Paraklete assisted or spoke for another in a court setting. The concept of *Paraklētos* has been variously translated to mean "Counselor," "Comforter," "Encourager," "Strengthener," "Helper," "Advocate," "Adviser," and "Ally".

Jesus Christ described the Holy Spirit as "another Advocate" or "Counselor" in John 14:16. However, Jesus Christ was the first Advocate or Paraclete (see 1 John 2:1). After His return to heaven, Jesus Christ sent the Holy Spirit to continue His teaching, love, and comfort-giving that He began during His earthly ministry (John 16:6-7; Acts 2). As Jesus Christ helped believers during His earthly ministry, so the Holy Spirit helped (and continues to help) believers after Jesus Christ's return to heaven.

CHAPTER 9
The Holy Spirit as Teacher and Revealer

26 "But the Helper, the Holy Spirit, whom the Father will send in My name, He will teach you all things, and bring to your remembrance all that I said to you." John 14:26 (NASB).

26 "But I will send you the Advocate—the Spirit of Truth. He will come to you from the Father and will testify all about Me." John 15:26 (NLT).

13 But when the Spirit of Truth comes, He will lead you into all truth. He will not speak His own words, but He will speak only what He hears, and He will tell you what is to come. 14 The Spirit of Truth will bring glory to Me, because He will take what I have to say and tell it to you. John 16:13-14 (NCV).

In the previous chapter, we discussed the role of the Holy Spirit as Advocate. The Holy Spirit strengthens the faith of those who believe completely in Jesus Christ as their savior, and helps believers confront the challenges and hostilities of a world that is often not amenable to Christian practice. However, the Holy Spirit does more than merely act as an advocate. It seeks to edify those who believe in Jesus Christ, continually building their heart love for the Trinity (God the Father, God the Son, and God the Holy Spirit).

The Holy Spirit is the Teacher and Revealer sent from God the Father and Jesus Christ (John 14:17, 26; John 15:26; John 16:13-15; 1 John 2:20, 27). He is the power of God that leads people into <u>all truth</u>. The Scriptures literally

call the Holy Spirit the Spirit of Truth (see John 15:26; John 16:13) because
He only speaks the truth about God and Jesus Christ. The Holy Spirit teaches
certain things to God's people and illuminates them so they can arrive at a
deeper understanding of God, His creation, and of circumstances.

> *27 But you have received the Holy Spirit, and He lives within
> you, in your hearts, so that you don't need anyone to teach
> you what is right. For He teaches you all things, and He is
> the Truth, and no liar; and so, just as He has said, you must
> live in Christ, never to depart from Him. 1 John 2:27 (TLB).*

As the Spirit of Truth, the Holy Spirit helps believers to discern and obey
the teachings of God (1 Corinthians 2:9-16). Jesus Christ promised to send
the Holy Spirit to teach His followers and to remind them of all that He had
taught (John 14:26). As a result, believers have Jesus Christ's Holy Spirit living
within them to keep them from going down a path of sin and to bring true
spiritual understanding. To remain in fellowship with Jesus Christ means, in
part, not being misled by any false teachings.

> *20 You gave them your good Spirit to teach them to live
> wisely. You never stinted with your manna, gave them
> plenty of water to drink. Nehemiah 9:20 (MSG).*

> *12 The Holy Spirit will teach you in that very hour
> what you ought to say. Luke 12:12 (NASB).*

> *17 He is the Holy Spirit, the Spirit who leads
> into all truth. John 14:17 (TLB).*

The Holy Spirit teaches and instructs believers regarding the truth of the Holy
Scriptures, in the process helping believers recognize truth and thereby better
understand God (see e.g., Exodus 33:2; Numbers 11:17; Nehemiah 9:20;
Isaiah 61:1; John 14:26; John 15:26; Acts 1:16; Acts 10:38; 2 Corinthians
1:21-22; Hebrews 9:8; Hebrews 10:15-17; 1 Peter 1:11-12; 1 John 2:20-23). As
God the Holy Spirit open and enlightened the minds and hearts of believers so
they may better understand the Holy Scriptures (Ephesians 1:17-18; Ephesians
3:18-19; 2 Corinthians 3:14-16; 4:6). Through the Holy Scriptures, believers
find understanding, wisdom, guidance, direction, and divine knowledge
(Isaiah 11:2). The Holy Spirit's work in providing this divine knowledge
is not a giving of new revelation. Instead, this spiritual understanding is a
work within believers by the Holy Spirit that enables believers to grasp the
Holy Scriptures as heard and read, and as explained by teachers and writers.

Only the Holy Spirit as the Searcher of the deep knowledge of God (1 Corinthians 2:10) can bring believers divine understanding, revelation, and wisdom of the things of God. When we are seeking help in understanding the Holy Scriptures, or simply pondering a decision in our lives, we as believers should always pray that the Holy Spirit will give us illumination, insight, and understanding.

> *10 But God has shown us these things through the Spirit. The Spirit searches out all things, even the deep secrets of God. 11 Who knows the thoughts that another person has? Only a person's spirit that lives within him knows his thoughts. It is the same with God. No one knows the thoughts of God except the Spirit of God. 12 Now we did not receive the spirit of the world, but we received the Spirit that is from God so that we can know all that God has given us. 13 And we speak about these things, not with words taught us by human wisdom but with words taught us by the Spirit. And so we explain spiritual truths to spiritual people.*
>
> *14 A person who does not have the Spirit does not accept the truths that come from the Spirit of God. That person thinks they are foolish and cannot understand them, because they can only be judged to be true by the Spirit. 1 Corinthians 2:10-14 (NCV).*

No one can fully understand everything about God (Romans 11:34). However, God graciously gives His Holy Spirit to believers so they can understand and know the wonderful things about Him that are hidden from the rest of the world (cp. John 16:13-14). Through the guidance of the Holy Spirit, believers can begin to know God's thoughts, gain more spiritual truths about God, and talk with Him through prayer. Through the Holy Spirit, believers begin to know God's thoughts and ways because the Holy Spirit speaks to believers' hearts (see Hebrews 3:7 and Hebrews 10:15). When we accept Jesus Christ as our Lord and Savior, the Holy Spirit gives us God's Spirit so we may understand God's deep secretes. These secrets can never be understood solely through philosophy or knowledge. *Only through God's own Holy Spirit can believers receive God's thoughts and wisdom* (see Matthew 11:25-27; 1 John 2:20, 27).

> *16 All Scripture is inspired by God and is useful to teach us what is true and to make us realize what is wrong in our lives. It corrects us when we are wrong and teaches us to do what is right. 2 Timothy 3:16 (NLT).*

> *20 Most of all, you must understand this: No prophecy in the Scriptures ever comes from the prophet's own interpretation. 21 No*

prophecy ever came from what a person wanted to say, but people led by the Holy Spirit spoke words from God. 2 Peter 1:20-21 (NCV).

The writers of the Holy Scriptures wrote The Holy Bible under the inspiration and the guidance of the Holy Spirit, who was providing them with the very thoughts and words of God. God revealed His Person and vision to certain believers, who wrote down His holy message for His people (2 Peter 1:20-21). Therefore, the Holy Scriptures are completely trustworthy because God was in control of their composition (see also Hebrews 4:12-13). When faced with difficult biblical passages, believers should always pray that the Holy Spirit will open their minds and hearts to understand and provide the needed insight to put God's Word into action in your life.

Prophecy is the main revelation of the Holy Spirit in the Old Testament. The Old Testament contains abundant examples of God's empowerment, inspiration, and informing of the prophets by giving them the revelation to speak through the Holy Spirit (e.g. see Ezekiel 3:1-4, 22-24; Haggai 2:5; Zechariah 4:6; Zechariah 7:12). Moreover, Joseph's dreams are perceived to be divinely inspired (Genesis 41:38). Also, King David proclaimed that "the Spirit of the Lord speaks" (2 Samuel 23:2) and the Prophet Zechariah announced the word of the Lord to Zerubbabel, "Not by might nor by power, but by My Spirit,' says the Lord of hosts" (Zechariah 4:6).

The tendency to exalt the Holy Spirit's role as the Inspirer of prophecy became steadily stronger in the period between the Old Testament and New Testament. When John the Baptist arrived to announce the arrival of the kingdom of God, the Spirit-inspired prophetic voice returned after a 400-year silence that had persisted since the prophet Malachi. In the past, the Spirit had been known as the Inspirer of prophetic writings, but after Haggai, Zechariah, and Malachi the Holy Spirit had been withdrawn and absent from Israel. Therefore, people had come to believe that the Holy Spirit was absent from the world. So, prior to the arrival of Jesus Christ, the Book of the Law written through the inspiration of the Holy Spirit became the Holy Spirit's only voice.

The New Testament was also written through the inspiration of the Holy Spirit. In the New Testament, at times the Holy Spirit reveals specific information to people. Examples of this include the Holy Spirit's revealing to Simeon that he will not die until he sees the Messiah (Luke 2:26), telling Agabus that a famine would occur (Acts 11:28), or letting Apostle Paul know what would happen in Jerusalem (Acts 20:23; 21:4). The Apostle Paul, one of the major writers of the New Testament, allowed the Holy Spirit's power to guide his words as he presented the message of the Gospel of Jesus Christ; he understood that human wisdom and philosophy by themselves will never bring people to Jesus Christ (see 1 Corinthians 1:17, 21; 2:2).

Effective work for God (as Apostle Paul keenly understood) starts and ends with complete reliance on God's Holy Spirit working from within. The Holy Spirit also gives power to our own words (as with the Apostle Paul) to bring glory to Jesus Christ and his message.

CHAPTER 10
Distinguishing True from False Spirit

13 "But when He, the Spirit of Truth, comes, He will guide you into all the truth; for He will not speak on His own initiative, but whatever He hears, He will speak; and He will disclose to you what is to come. 14 He will glorify Me, for He will take of Mine and will disclose it to you." John 16:13-14 (NASB).

How to recognize the truth of the Holy Spirit? How can one distinguish true spiritual inspiration from false or fake inspiration? These questions have been asked and agonized over by many people, including Biblical scholars.

Jesus Christ promised to send the Holy Spirit to teach His followers and to remind them of the truths of His message (John 14:26). As a result, believers of Jesus Christ have the Holy Spirit within them ("the Anointing") so they will not stray from the teachings of Jesus Christ. Moreover, believers have the Spirit-inspired Holy Bible to verify and test any questionable teachings.

Precisely defining the Holy Spirit

26 But I will send you the Comforter—the Holy Spirit, the source of all Truth. He will come to you from the Father and will tell you all about Me. John 15:26 (TLB).

It is this more precise definition of the Holy Spirit found in John 15:26 that provides believers with answers to the frequent question: how to recognize the experience of the Spirit to be such. The answer is partly that the Holy

Spirit is to be identified as the Spirit that tells the truth and teaches the genuine message of God in Jesus Christ (see John 15:26; 16:13-14; Acts 5:32; 1 Corinthians 12:3; 1 John 4:2; 5:7-8; Revelation 19:10). The Holy Spirit always reflects, reveals, and teaches the *humility* and *truth* of Jesus Christ.

False prophets

> *15 Beware of false prophets who come disguised as harmless sheep but are really vicious wolves. 16 You can identify them by their fruit, that is, by the way they act. Can you pick grapes from thornbushes, or figs from thistles? 17 A good tree produces good fruit, and a bad tree produces bad fruit. 18 A good tree can't produce bad fruit, and a bad tree can't produce good fruit. 19 So every tree that does not produce good fruit is chopped down and thrown into the fire. 20 Yes, just as you can identify a tree by its fruit, so you can identify people by their actions. Matthew 7:15-20 (NLT). See Matthew 12:33-37 and Luke 6:43-45.*

False teachers, prophets, and spirits are as common today as during the Old Testament periods (see Matthew 24:11, 24; Acts 20:28-35; Revelation 13:11-18; Revelation 16:13; Revelation 19:20; Revelation 20:10). These false prophets or spirits do not teach people to obey God's Holy Scriptures and live according to His written Word, but only speak tell people what they want to hear. God still speaks to His people, but we must be careful before saying that someone is God's spokesperson. Clearly, the Word of the Lord is more than simply every message delivered in some sort of excitement. So, the Holy Scriptures provide believers tests or warning signs to evaluate a true Spirit and prophecy from God:

1. Always evaluate the speaker's actions, behavior, and lifestyle to see whether they conform to God's Holy Scriptures. The speaker may appear to speak God's message, but not live according to God's principles.

2. Verify every message you hear, even if the person who brings the message says it's from God. You must assure yourself that the message matches what God says in his Holy Word. Sadly, some speakers "water down" or dilute God's Holy Message, making it more palatable but in the process ignoring God's truth in the Bible. Even worse, some speakers encourage listeners, often subtly, to disobey God and God's Holy Scriptures.

3. See whether or not the prophecy or predictions made by the speaker come true.

4. Assess the quality of inspiration. Unfortunately, some speakers tend to be prideful, self-serving, and appeal to the desires of the audience instead of being true to God's Holy Word.

5. Confirm what the speaker believes about Jesus Christ (e.g., Does the speaker teach that Jesus Christ is fully God and fully man?).

Some Scriptures you can consult are Deuteronomy 13:1-5; Deuteronomy 18:22; Isaiah 44:7-8; Jeremiah 23:14; Micah 3:5; Matthew 3:8-10; Matthew 13:8; Matthew 21:43; Galatians 5:19-23; James 2:14-26; 1 John 2:19; 1 John 3:23-24; 1 John 4:6.

Just as the fruit indicates the nature of a tree, so a person's life reveals either a true heart for God or an imposter. Good prophets and teachers consistently demonstrate good behavior and live according to precepts of high moral character. This is their attempt to live out the truths of God's Holy Scriptures. Most often, false teachers and prophets sound religious but are motivated by money, fame, or power. Their teachings minimize God and glorify themselves.

Moses warned the Israelites in Deuteronomy 13:1-5 that attractive leaders are not always led by God. New ideas from people who are inspiring and charismatic may sound good. However, the Holy Scriptures teach believers to judge leaders and speakers by whether or not their teachings are consistent and in line with God's Word. When any person (whether a leader, a close friend, or a family member) claims to speak for God, check the speaker to determine if the teachings are true, focused on God, and consistent with what you already know to be true from the Holy Bible.

God's Holy Scriptures are not always pleasurable, but sometimes challenging and hard. The Scriptures speak against sin, evil, pride, hate, and selfishness (and, in general, self-oriented behavior) among other things. Refusing to listen to and obey God's true Word as found in the Scriptures can be destructive and costly. Everyone, including Bible teachers, has listened and read the Holy Scriptures selectively, often focusing on Scriptures that seem to support our present lifestyle while ignoring the true demands of the Scriptures. However, if we accept God's Holy Scriptures completely, we have an opportunity to live life to the fullest in accordance to God's will.

> *¹ Beloved, do not believe every spirit, but test the spirits to see whether they are from God, because many false prophets have gone out into the world. 1 John 4:1 (NASB).*

Sadly, some people believe everything they read or hear. The Holy Scriptures are clear: "do not believe every spirit, but test the spirits." This means that, as believers, we should not believe everything we hear just because someone says it is a message inspired by God. Some people speak the truth while directing you toward God, but others speak convincingly while directing you wrongly, away from God and His Holy Word.

Accepting the Holy Spirit's teachings

> *¹⁹ Do not smother the Holy Spirit. ²⁰ Do not scoff at those who prophesy, ²¹ but test everything that is said to be sure it is true, and if it is, then accept it. ²² Keep away from every kind of evil. 1 Thessalonians 5:19-22 (TLB).*

God wants believers to examine speech (testimony) carefully for its truth. Believers must not simply dismiss all teachings. It is true that false prophets and spirits are still around today. In order not to be deceived, believers must be perceptive, shrewd, sensitive, and discerning. Moreover, believers can defeat false spirits, prophecy, and teaching by pouring out our hearts to God in prayer and by diligently studying His Word. Through the guidance of the Holy Spirit, believers can **_ALWAYS_** carefully test ideas and speeches against the **_TRUTH of God's Word_**. God never contradicts Himself. If someone says something contrary to the Holy Bible, it is not God's Word. If the message is truly from God, the message will be consistent with God's teachings. (See 1 Corinthians 12:10; 1 Thessalonians 5:21; 1 John 4:1-3; Revelation 2:20).

Our world is filled with false voices that claim to speak for God. Believers of Jesus Christ should have faith, but they should not be gullible, immature, naïve, and easy to fool. With the help of the Holy Spirit, believers have God-inspired Holy Scriptures to test questionable teachings and to distinguish or discern truth from error. The Holy Scriptures are our safeguard against false, questionable, and deceptive teaching from non-believers (2 Timothy 4:2-4; 1 Timothy 1:4-7; cp. 2 Peter 3:16). God Himself has confirmed the Holy Bible through the *inward* witness of the Holy Spirit to our hearts. The Holy Spirit brings a growing knowledge of the truth and love about God and His Son, Jesus Christ, and convicts the world of sin (John 16:8-11) while offering each of us the opportunity to cleanse ourselves in the midst of the corrupt world. Most important, the Scriptures equip believers to do good, strengthening their faith and love.

CHAPTER 11
The Holy Spirit Empowers the Church

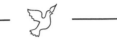

³ Make every effort to keep yourselves <u>united</u> in the Spirit, binding yourselves <u>together with peace</u>. ⁴ For there is one body and one Spirit, just as you have been called to one glorious hope for the future. ⁵ There is one Lord, one faith, one baptism, ⁶ and one God and Father, who is over all and in all and living through all. ⁷ However, He has given each one of us a special gift through the generosity of Christ... ¹¹ Now these are the gifts Christ gave to the church: the apostles, the prophets, the evangelists, and the pastors and teachers. ¹² Their responsibility is to equip [prepare] God's people to do His work [service] and build up the church, the body of Christ. Ephesians 4:3-7, 11-12 (NLT).

God gives each member of the body of Christ *gifts* to serve to God and others and to build up the body of Christ (Ephesians 3:10; Ephesians 4:11-16; Romans 12:6-8; 1 Corinthians 12:4-11, 28). God never intended His spiritual gifts to be used for an individual's personal benefit, or to bring division and strife among His people. Sadly, different spiritual gifts can divide people and churches, as was the case in Corinthians, but God never intended such results. Instead, God generously provides His gifts to His children to serve and love others and to build the church up through unity and peace (1 Peter 4:10-11). Each believer's gift from the Holy Spirit is different, but together these gifts help spread the Good News of God's love through Jesus Christ and God's loving grace and forgiveness.

The Apostle Paul called these God-given spiritual gifts *charismata* (gifts which are specific manifestations of *charis* or grace (1 Corinthians 12:4)), and also *pneumatika* or God's *pneuma* (spiritual gifts as specific demonstrations of the energy of the Holy Spirit (1 Corinthians 12:1)). Since the Holy Spirit is the One that manifests, or reveals God's presence in the world, the Apostle Paul simply calls spiritual gifts "manifestations" of the Holy Spirit (1 Corinthians 12:7). When spiritual gifts are active within the church body, God's presence is visible.

> *⁴ There are different kinds of spiritual gifts, but the same Spirit is the source of them all. ⁵ There are different kinds of service, but we serve the same Lord. ⁶ God works in different ways, but it is the same God who does the work in all of us. ⁷ A spiritual gift is given to each of us so we can help each other.*
> *1 Corinthians 12:4-7 (NLT).*

The significance of a person's spiritual gifts has been debated and questioned among fellow Christians. Despite the debate, three certainties stand out.

First, spiritual gifts are to be used to express, celebrate, display, and communicate Jesus Christ and His love. The New Testament provides that spiritual gifts, when rightly used, should build up and love fellow Christians and Jesus Christ's churches.

Second, all spiritual gifts given from God through Jesus Christ are of equal respect and importance and should be properly used within the body of Christ (see 1 Corinthians 7:7; 1 Corinthians 12:8-10; Ephesians 4:11; 1 Peter 4:10-11).

Third, every believer is given a gift from Jesus Christ to be used in the church body. **No believer is without a spiritual gift** (1 Corinthians 12:7; Ephesians 4:7). Jesus Christ has generously distributed spiritual gifts to believers to help empower, build, and carry on the mission of the church. The Holy Scriptures encourages Christians to find, develop, and fully use whatever gifting given by the Holy Spirit for service to God through Jesus Christ.

> *¹⁹ Do not quench the Spirit. ²⁰ Do not despise prophecies. ²¹ Test all things; hold fast what is good. ²² Abstain from every form of evil.*
> *1 Thessalonians 5:19-22 (NKJV).*

The Holy Scriptures warns believers not to "quench the Spirit", which means that we should not ignore nor discourage spiritual gifts. Some types of spiritual gifts (such as prophecy and speaking in tongues) have caused controversy.[2] The Holy Scriptures teach that true spiritual gifts must be cultivated and encouraged within the body of Christ (2 Timothy 1:6). Regardless of how controversial or not a particular spiritual gift is, *any gift that benefits and encourages the body of Christ* must never be smothered and ignored.

Any spiritual gift that does not build up and encourage the body of Christ is not a gift of the Holy Spirit. Nevertheless, all spiritual gifts should be carefully checked out and tested to assure their truth and alignment with God's Holy Scriptures. The Epistles of Apostle Paul (due to their specificity concerning the nature of spiritual gifts) can help in this endeavor. In his Epistles, the Apostle Paul referred to about twenty different spiritual gifts, including such things as preaching, teaching, and leadership. But most biblical scholars agree that these spiritual gifts are not a complete list but only representative of the various spiritual gifts given by God. As we today can recognize within the church, many spiritual gifts were not mentioned by the Apostle Paul, such as the gift of music, working with young people, and counseling. Nevertheless, the list of spiritual gifts specifically found in the New Testament include:

> [7] *A spiritual gift is given to each of us so we can <u>help each other</u>.* [8] *To one person the Spirit gives the ability to give wise advice; to another the same Spirit gives a message of special knowledge.* [9] *The same Spirit gives great faith to another, and to someone else the one Spirit gives the gift of healing.* [10] *He gives one person the power to perform miracles, and another the ability to prophesy. He gives someone else the ability to discern whether a message is from the Spirit of God or from another spirit. Still another person is given the ability to speak in unknown languages, while another is given the ability to interpret what is being said.* [11] *It is the one and only Spirit who distributes all these gifts. He alone decides which gift each person should have. 1 Corinthians 12:7-11 (NLT).*

> [27] *<u>Together</u> you are the body of Christ, and each one of you is a [necessary] part of that body.* [28] *In the church God has given a place first to apostles, second to prophets, and third to teachers. Then God has given a place to those who do miracles, those who have gifts of healing, those who can help others, those who are able to govern, and those who can speak in different languages.*

---

2   While the experience of being filled with the Holy Spirit may result in the gift of speaking in tongues, or in the use of some other gifts that had not previously been experienced, it also may come without the gift of speaking in tongues. In fact, many Christians throughout history have been empowered with the Holy Spirit in a fashion that did not involve the ability to speak in tongues.

29 Not all are apostles. Not all are prophets. Not all are teachers. Not all do miracles. 30 Not all have gifts of healing. Not all speak in different languages. Not all interpret those languages. 31 But you should truly want to have the greater gifts. And now I will show you the best way of all. 1 I may speak in different languages of people or even angels. But if I do not have <u>love</u>, I am only a noisy bell or a crashing cymbal. 2 I may have the gift of prophecy. I may understand all the secret things of God and have all knowledge, and I may have faith so great I can move mountains. But even with all these things, if I do not have <u>love</u>, then I am nothing. 3 I may give away everything I have, and I may even give my body as an offering to be burned. But I gain nothing if I do not have <u>love</u>. 1 Corinthians 12:27-13:3 (NCV).

3 For by the grace given me [Apostle Paul] I say to every one of you: Do not think of yourself more highly than you ought, but rather think of yourself with sober judgment, in accordance with the measure of faith God has given you. 4 Just as each of us has one body with many members, and these members do not all have the same function, 5 so in Christ we who are many form one body, and each member belongs to all the others. 6 We have different gifts, according to the grace given us. If a man's gift is prophesying, let him use it in proportion to his faith. 7 If it is serving, let him serve; if it is teaching, let him teach; 8 if it is encouraging, let him encourage; if it is contributing to the needs of others, let him give generously; if it is leadership, let him govern diligently; if it is showing mercy, let him do it cheerfully. 9 <u>Love</u> must be sincere. Hate what is evil; cling to what is good. 10 Be devoted to one another in brotherly <u>love</u>. Honor one another above yourselves. 11 Never be lacking in zeal, but keep your spiritual fervor, serving the Lord. Romans 12:3-11 (NIV).

11 Now these are the gifts Christ gave to the church: the apostles, the prophets, the evangelists, and the pastors and teachers. Ephesians 4:11 (NLT).

10 God has given each of you a gift from His great variety of spiritual gifts. Use them well <u>to serve one another</u>. 11 Do you have the gift of speaking? Then speak as though God himself were speaking through you. Do you have the gift of helping others? Do it with all the strength and energy that God supplies. Then everything you do will bring glory to God through Jesus Christ. All glory and power to Him forever and ever! Amen. 1 Peter 4:10-11 (NLT).

The Holy Spirit decides which spiritual gift (or gifts) a person receives; therefore, no person can take credit for what God has freely given (1 Corinthians 12:11). With regard to any spiritual gift, believers must simply say that the Holy Spirit "apportions each one individually as He wills" (1 Corinthians 12:11). Yet as believers, we are responsible to use and sharpen our gifts to serve others and glorify God. All the spiritual work believers do for God is only God's Holy Spirit working through them (see 2 Corinthians 4:7; Galatians 2:8, 20; Philippians 2:13; 1 John 3:24). *All true believers of Jesus Christ* (not just one or two specially anointed individuals) have the Holy Spirit through faith in Jesus Christ; this was part of the new covenant described in the New Testament. Moreover, *all true believers* and not just a particular prophet may be used by the Holy Spirit as ministers of God's grace (See Romans 8:9; 1 Corinthians 2:12; 1 Corinthians 12:7-11).

In the Old Testament, the Holy Spirit was given to selected individuals rather than to all of God's children. When the Holy Spirit came to a person, He brought with Him one or more gifts that equipped that person to serve God by serving Israel. Examples of the Holy Spirit's giving of gifts includes: Bezaleel, who was given the gift of craftsmanship (Exodus 31:2-3); Othniel, who was equipped to be a judge (Judges 3:9-10); Gideon, who was given military skills (Judges 6:34); Samson, who was given physical strength (Judges 14:6,19); Saul, who was given political skills (1 Samuel 10:6); and Micah, who was given prophetic gifts (Micah 3:8).

Nonetheless, the Old Testament provides a background for the Christian understanding of spiritual gifts. The believers' view of spiritual gifts begins with Jesus Christ because He was the special bearer of the Holy Spirit (Mark 1:10). The Holy Spirit directed and empowered Jesus Christ for His ministry (Luke 4:14-18). Jesus Christ promised believers that they, too, would receive the Holy Spirit one day and that the Spirit would guide them (see John 14:16).

> [17] *For the Kingdom of God is not a matter of what we eat or drink, but of living a life of goodness and peace and joy in the Holy Spirit.* [18] *If you serve Christ with this attitude, you will please God, and others will approve of you, too.* [19] *So then, let us aim for harmony in the church and try to build each other up.*
> Romans 14:17-19 (NLT).

There are many different spiritual gifts people receive from God and some people have more than one spiritual gift. Spiritual gifts given by the Holy Spirit are to be used to serve and help the needs of the body of Christ (that is, the local church) and not for our own exclusive enjoyment. Sadly, some people see spiritual gifts as some form of special power to lord over, manipulate, and crush people. Or, believers' gifts can lead to arrogance or pride ("I have the gift of speaking" or "I have the gift of prophecy"). Moreover, some believers tend to think individualistically, and believe their special talents should be used exclusively to please and satisfy themselves. In reality, a terrible misuse of spiritual gifts occurs when they become symbols of power that cause rivalries and division within the church; spiritual gifts should never be used in a divisive manner. In the body of Christ, **all believers or members** have a spiritual gift from God to build up and unify the church and to help the church function more effectively. Through our gifts and special abilities, God receives glory and praise as others see Jesus Christ in us and praise Him for the help and good deeds they receive (see Matthew 5:16).

> [1] *Let love be your highest goal! But you should also desire the special abilities the Spirit gives—especially the ability to prophesy. 1 Corinthians 14:1 (NLT).*

> [29] *"The most important commandment is this: '... [30] And you must love the LORD your God with all your heart, all your soul, all your mind, and all your strength.' [31] The second is equally important: 'Love your neighbor as yourself.' No other commandment is greater than these." Mark 12:29-31 (NLT).*

> [12] *My command is this: Love each other as I have loved you. John 15:12 (NIV).*

> [7] *Dear friends, let us continue to love one another, for love comes from God. Anyone who loves is a child of God and knows God. [8] But anyone who does not love does not know God, for God is love. 1 John 4:7-8 (NLT).*

The gifts of God's Holy Spirit benefit, encourage, and build up the body of Christ. This explains why love and the gift of prophecy are ranked so highly by the Apostle Paul. Love is more important than all the spiritual gifts in the church body. Love serves God and enhances the spiritual growth of the church as a whole (1 Corinthians 13, 14). Spiritual gifts are worth very little to the body of Christ without love because love makes our gifts effective. Any spiritual gift that does not build up the body of Christ is unlikely to be a gift of the Holy Spirit (Matthew 7:15-23).

³¹ So whether you eat or drink or whatever
you do, do it all for the glory of God.
1 Corinthians 10:31 (NIV).

Regardless of which spiritual gift a believer receives from God, all gifts are to be used to glorify and love God and serve and love people. God never intended to use our spiritual gifts to selfishly serve and love ourselves, but to serve and love God and our neighbors. In addition, the Holy Scriptures are very clearly the most valuable gift of all. The Apostle Paul's answer is clear: the one gift all believers must have is LOVE (1 Corinthians 12:31-13:1). Love is the greatest spiritual gift. Jesus Christ said that with love a person fulfills the entire Law (See Matthew 22:36-40; Romans 13:10). If we have all other spiritual gifts and yet do not have love, we have nothing. Love assures that our spiritual gifts from God will not be used selfishly or arrogantly. *God is love.*

Moreover, some believers tend to distinguish spiritual gifts from natural abilities, but (at least in the Scriptures) this distinction did not occur to Apostle Paul. In listing spiritual gifts, the Apostle Paul proposes that whatever skills a believer has are given by God, and should be used in God's service so that we may love one another. All ministry must be performed through the Holy Spirit.

²⁵ Jesus called all the followers together and said, "You know
that the rulers of the non-Jewish people love to show their power
over the people. And their important leaders love to use all their
authority. ²⁶ But it should not be that way among you. Whoever
wants to become great among you must serve the rest of you like a
servant. ²⁷ Whoever wants to become first among you must serve
the rest of you like a slave. ²⁸ In the same way, the Son of Man
did not come to be served. He came to serve others and to give
his life as a ransom for many people." Matthew 20:25-28 (NCV).

Jesus Christ's life and teaching centered on loving and serving others. He held children in His arms, healed the sick, washed the disciples' feet, and died for the sins of the entire world. Following Jesus Christ also means receiving this same power to serve. As believers, we are called to be servants of Jesus Christ. As Jesus Christ served, believers are to use their spiritual gifts to serve others. God wants every believer to use his or her spiritual gifts to serve one another and not to "lord it over" other people (Matthew 20:25-28). This usefulness of every believer in the service of God is sometimes called the "priesthood of all believers" (1 Peter 2:5-9; Revelation 1:6; Revelation 5:10; see Exodus 19:6;

Isaiah 61:6; Revelation 20:6). Not everyone has the same role, but all have the same calling to use their spiritual gifts in God's service.

> *12 The human body has many parts, but the many parts make up one whole body. So it is with the body of Christ. 13 Some of us are Jews, some are Gentiles, some are slaves, and some are free. But we have all been baptized into one body by one Spirit, and we all share the same Spirit.*
> *1 Corinthians 12:12-13 (NLT).*

> *25 The way God designed our bodies is a model for understanding our lives together as a church: every part dependent on every other part, the parts we mention and the parts we don't, 26 the parts we see and the parts we don't. If one part hurts, every other part is involved in the hurt, and in the healing. If one part flourishes, every other part enters into the exuberance.*
> *1 Corinthians 12:25-26 (MSG).*

At Pentecost, the Holy Spirit created a new community called the church. The community was marketed by unity (Acts 2:44-47). The Apostle Paul attributed the unity within the church community to the Holy Spirit's presence (2 Corinthians 13:14). He encouraged the church to maintain the unity of the Spirit in the bond of peace (Ephesians 4:3).

The local church (also called the body of Christ) plays an important work in continuing the work of Jesus Christ to the world. Every member in the church plays an important role in building up and equipping the local body of Christ. Despite formal titles or formal positions, all members of the local church are equally important for equipping, building, and encouraging one another (Ephesians 4:11-13). The body of Christ grows to maturity, full of love and perfectly, as each member uses his or her spiritual gift (Ephesians 4:16).

All true believers in Jesus Christ belong to one body united under Jesus Christ Himself, who is the head of the church (see 1 Corinthians 12:12-26). Unity should be present within the body of Christ, but believers must work at this unity. Unity will not just happen; the church has many different types of people from a variety of backgrounds who possess diverse gifts and abilities. All believers have one thing in common in spite of these differences: baptism by the Holy Spirit through faith in Jesus Christ.

> *2 Be humble and gentle. Be patient with each other, making allowance for each other's faults because of your love. 3*

Try always to be led along together by the Holy Spirit and
so be at peace with one another. Ephesians 4:2-3 (TLB).

[19] *"Again I say to you, that if two of you agree on earth about*
anything that they may ask, it shall be done for them by My Father
who is in heaven. [20] *For where two or three have gathered together*
in My name, I am there in their midst." Matthew 18:19-20 (NASB).

In the body of believers (or the church), the genuine agreement of two people allows Jesus Christ's spirit to be with them. In the early church, the Holy Spirit provided the unifying bond that allowed the work of spreading the Gospel to be carried out. On the decisive day of Pentecost, when the disciples were <u>united</u> and <u>expectant</u> as they <u>gathered for prayer</u>, the Holy Spirit came and filled the gathered believers with God's power from on high (see also Jude 1:19-20). Moreover, the early Christian church was able to share their possessions and property because of the unity brought by the Holy Spirit working in and through the believers' lives.

Believers should not think that any one person is totally independent and requires no help from others. More to the point, no believer should ever feel excused from the work of helping others. The church (the body of Jesus Christ) functions only when its believing members work together for the common good (John 13:34-35). True believers of Jesus Christ are not proud or arrogant but humbly help and serve others.

God's Holy Spirit brings fellowship, unity, and love to those who believe in Jesus Christ. To build unity within the church is one of the Holy Spirit's important roles. Believers can assist in this by focusing on obeying and imitating God, rather than on our own sometimes narrow sphere of concern. The Holy Spirit may bring unity. But believers must also be willing to be led and to do their part to keep the peace among brothers and sisters in Jesus Christ.

The church is a body with Jesus Christ as the head and each believer as a member (Ephesians 4:15-16). To coin a metaphor, the Holy Scriptures describe the church as a living, spiritual house, with Jesus Christ as the foundation and cornerstone and each believer as a stone (1 Peter 2:4-8). The goal of every church should be that God will place His Holy Spirit into its body of believers (Ezekiel 37:14), who form a community.

God does not want the church damaged, spoiled, or ruined by division, envy, controversy, jealousy, or other sins. Believers of Jesus Christ represent Him to the world, and their conduct and relationships with each other should reflect His image. When division, jealousy, and infighting occur, believers are not faithfully representing the humble love of Jesus Christ (John 13:35; 1 John 3:11).

> *¹ Is there any encouragement from belonging to Christ? Any comfort from His love? Any fellowship together in the Spirit? Are your hearts tender and compassionate? ² Then make me truly happy by agreeing wholeheartedly with each other, loving one another, and working together with one mind and purpose. Philippians 2:1-2 (NLT). See also Acts 2:42.*

God's amazing eternal plan through Jesus Christ is to unite Gentiles [non-Jews] with Jews in a new group of people called the church (Ephesians 1:9; Ephesians 2:14-22; Ephesians 3:6). With this plan, Gentiles are no longer "foreigners or strangers", but "fellow citizens with God's people and also members of his household" (Ephesians 2:14-22). The church is part of God's plan to bring everything in heaven and on earth under the authority of Jesus Christ (Ephesians 1:9-10). The church is the Israel of God — the "new people of God" (Galatians 6:16) and God's family (Ephesians 2:19)—the "household of God" (1 Timothy 3:15). The church is a Temple of God (Ephesians 2:21-22) where God lives by His Holy Spirit (Ephesians 2:22; Ephesians 4:6; 1 Corinthians 3:16-17; 2 Corinthians 6:16; Colossians 1:27). Within the church, God wants all His people — comprised of different ethnic groups — to be a community of harmony, unity, faith, love and peace, bound together by the Holy Spirit (Ephesians 4:2-15; Romans 8:29). Most importantly, God wants people to become like and imitate Jesus Christ (Ephesians 4:24-5:1).

CHAPTER 12
Daily Guidance of the Holy Spirit

¹² So, my brothers and sisters, we must not be ruled by our sinful selves or live the way our sinful selves want. ¹³ If you use your lives to do the wrong things your sinful selves want, you will die spiritually. But if you use the Spirit's help to stop doing the wrong things you do with your body, you will have true life. ¹⁴ The true children of God are those who let God's Spirit lead them. ¹⁵ The Spirit we received does not make us slaves again to fear; it makes us children of God. With that Spirit we cry out, "Father." ¹⁶ And the Spirit Himself joins with our spirits to say we are God's children. Romans 8:12-16 (NCV).

The Apostle Paul divides people into two categories — those who let themselves be guided by their sinful natures and those who are guided by the Holy Spirit (Romans 8:5-6). All humankind by birth falls into the first category due to the original sin of Adam and Eve in the Garden of Eden in Genesis 3. However, through faith in the life and Person of Jesus Christ, a believer of Jesus Christ joins the second category.

Our human body is controlled by two forces struggling and fighting within us — the Holy Spirit of God borne of belief and trust in Jesus Christ as our savior, and the sinful nature inherited at birth from Adam and Eve (see Genesis 4:7; Romans 7:14-25; 1 Peter 2:11). To defeat this raging war within our bodies and to control sin and evil in our bodies and minds, believers must live each and every day obeying Jesus Christ's teaching, by prayer and faith, and living by the Holy Spirit. ___Daily___ believers must purposefully and deliberately choose to center their lives on God and God's guidelines as stated in His Holy Scriptures. The Holy Bible can be considered God's "life guidelines"; God's Holy Spirit gives believers strength to obey God's teachings as found in the Scriptures.

The Holy Spirit helps believers defeat and control sin in their bodies and minds by giving believers a heart desire to obey God. No human being can defeat, control, or master sin through his or her own strength. At the same time, believers must be mindful and avoid confusing their personal feelings with the Holy Spirit's guidance. Being led and directed by the Holy Spirit involves the desire to hear, the willingness to obey God's Holy Word in His Scriptures, and the sensitivity to discern between your feelings and God's promptings.

> [16] *So I say, live by the Spirit, and you will not gratify the desires of the sinful nature.* [17] *For the sinful nature desires what is contrary to the Spirit, and the Spirit what is contrary to the sinful nature. They are in conflict with each other, so that you do not do what you want.* [18] *But if you are led by the Spirit, you are not under law.* [19] *The Acts of the sinful nature are obvious: sexual immorality, impurity and debauchery;* [20] *idolatry and witchcraft; hatred, discord, jealousy, fits of rage, selfish ambition, dissensions, factions* [21] *and envy; drunkenness, orgies, and the like. I warn you, as I did before, that those who live like this will not inherit the kingdom of God.* [22] *But the fruit of the Spirit is love, joy, peace, patience, kindness, goodness, faithfulness,* [23] *gentleness and self-control. Against such things there is no law.* [24] *Those who belong to Christ Jesus have crucified the sinful nature with its passions and desires.* [25] *Since we live by the Spirit, let us keep in step with the Spirit.* [26] *Let us not become conceited, provoking and envying each other. Galatians 5:16-26 (NIV).*

In Galatians 5:19-26, the Apostle Paul gives two lists that contrast a human life dominated by the sinful nature of neglecting God and others (Galatians 5:19-21) with a life guided and controlled by God's Holy Spirit of living and loving God and others (Galatians 5:22-26). A life that follows the natural, sinful nature seeks to please and gratify oneself only. These sins include such things as:

- Idolatry (the worship of false gods);
- Sorcery and witchcraft;
- Sexual immorality;
- Hostility (arises from angry pride and arrogance);

- Selfish ambition (selfishness or self-centered actions);
- Quarreling (stirring up discord and looking for a fight);
- Outbursts of anger (or fits of rage);
- Drunkenness;
- Impatience;
- Destructive, hateful, or evil behavior;
- Impurity;
- Lust;
- Hatred;
- Jealousy;
- Envy;
- Murder;
- Wild living;
- Cheating;
- Adultery;
- Homosexuality;
- Greed;
- Stealing; and
- Lying

This list is only representative of the potential vices that comprise the sinful nature. Sadly, people living that sort of life are not living by God's Holy Spirit and their actions reveal they have no relationship with God. Eventually, living a sinful life leads to spiritual decay, depression, and death.

The Holy Spirit brings forth the "fruit of the Spirit" within a believer. The qualities of the fruit of the Spirit reflect the very nature of God Himself. Only by and through the Holy Spirit is a believer of Jesus Christ able to "put to death the deeds of the body" and grow in personal holiness (Romans 8:13). The genuine and lasting presence of the Holy Spirit is revealed in the fruits of the Spirit (see Matthew 7:15-20; 1 Corinthians 14:12, 26).[3] The fruits of the Spirit provide evidence that the Holy Spirit is at work in a person or in a group of people. Galatians 5:22-23 lists the "fruit of the Spirit" as:

- Love (the greatest fruit that encompasses all the other fruits of the Spirit (1 Corinthians 13:4-7);
- Joy (that does not depend on life's circumstances);

---

3   The phrases "slain in the Spirit" or "slaying in the Spirit" are not used in the Holy Scriptures. However, there are various places throughout the Holy Scriptures where people fall to the ground in the holy presence of God (see Genesis 15:12; Exodus 40:35; Daniel 8:27; John 18:6; Acts 9:4; Revelation 1:17).

- Peace (creates internal well-being and heart calmness);
- Patience (tolerance or "long-suffering" towards other people, even under unfavorable circumstances);
- Kindness (means generosity and a giving spirit);
- Goodness;
- Faithfulness (or faith and fidelity in our relationships);
- Gentleness; and
- Self-control

> *15 So be very careful how you live. Do not live like those who are not wise, but live wisely. 16 Use every chance you have for doing good, because these are evil times. 17 So do not be foolish but learn what the Lord wants you to do. 18 Do not be drunk with wine, which will ruin you, but be filled with the Spirit.*
> *Ephesians 5:15-18 (NCV).*

When a person is born again by accepting Jesus Christ as Lord and Savior, God's Holy Spirit empowers a person with God's moral goodness (see John 3:6; John 14:17-23; 2 Corinthians 5:21; and 1 Peter 1:22-23). As we obey Jesus Christ who guides us by His Spirit, we will live a life of love for God and others with good deeds and actions. Living by God's Holy Spirit results in Christ-like behavior, and helps reap God's abundant rewards from one's work (Galatians 6:6-10). Yet, living to please God is only possible through the power of the Holy Spirit (Galatians 3:3; Galatians 5:16).

The Holy Spirit should always control a believer's life (Acts 2:15-18). Living according to the Holy Spirit means wholeheartedly and humbly giving every part of our lives—emotional, physical, social, intellectual, and vocational, not just spiritual—to God and His Holy Spirit. As believers of Jesus Christ, we must daily commit our sinful tendencies and habits to God's control, willingly nail our sinful nature to the cross, and moment by moment draw on the Holy Spirit's power to overcome sin and evil (see Galatians 2:20; Galatians 6:14). We should submit ourselves daily to the Holy Spirit's leading and draw constantly on His power.

> *5 In view of all this, make every effort to respond to God's promises. Supplement your faith with a generous provision of moral excellence, and moral excellence with knowledge, 6 and knowledge with self-control, and self-control with patient endurance, and patient endurance with godliness, 7 and godliness with brotherly affection, and brotherly affection with love for everyone. 2 Peter 1:5-7 (NLT).*

True and everlasting spiritual life means our human effort and both living by the Holy Spirit's power and trust in God. The Holy Spirit produces fruit that is good, productive, loving, uplifting, giving, holy, patient, nurturing, and caring. Nevertheless, the Holy Scriptures also encourages believers to always to do good and right by the Holy Spirit's guidance. As believers, we must live a life of moral excellence that pleases God. Ultimately, being filled with God's Holy Spirit produces a higher and lasting joy. This joy cures depression, monotony, or tension (Romans 5:1-2; Colossians 3:16-17).

The Holy Spirit makes a believer righteous and holy through faith in Jesus Christ (Romans 3:21-31). God's Holy Spirit gives believers the will and the power to live a life that pleases God and to obey His Law. Those who walk with the Holy Spirit and follow His leading each day will avoid sin because God's Holy Spirit leads, guides, and controls people's hearts away from sin and to God. The Holy Spirit directs and guides believers of Jesus Christ to fulfill God's Law because the essence of God's Law is the fruit of the Spirit (love, joy, peace, patience, kindness, goodness, faithfulness, gentleness, and self-control).

Remain in Jesus Christ, and He will remain in you

[1] "I am [Jesus Christ] the True Grapevine, and My Father is the Gardener. [2] He [God the Father] cuts off every branch of Mine that doesn't produce fruit, and He prunes the branches that do bear fruit so they will produce even more. [3] You have already been pruned and purified by the message I have given you. [4] Remain in Me, and I will remain in you. For a branch cannot produce fruit if it is severed from the vine, and you cannot be fruitful unless you remain in Me. [5] Yes, I am the Vine; you are the branches. Those who remain in Me, and I in them, will produce much fruit. For apart from Me you can do nothing. [6] Anyone who does not remain in Me is thrown away like a useless branch and withers. Such branches are gathered into a pile to be burned. [7] But if you remain in Me [Jesus Christ] and My Words remain in you, you may ask for anything you want, and it will be granted! [8] When you produce much fruit, you are My true disciples. This brings great glory to My Father. [9] I have loved you even as the Father has loved Me. Remain in My love. [10] When you **obey** My commandments, **you remain in My love**, just as I obey My Father's commandments and remain in His love. [11] I have told you these things so that you will be filled with My joy. Yes, your joy will overflow! [12] This is My commandment: Love each other in the

same way I have loved you. ¹³ There is no greater love than to lay down one's life for one's friends. ¹⁴ You are My friends if you do what I command. ¹⁵ I no longer call you slaves, because a master doesn't confide in his slaves. Now you are My friends, since I have told you everything the Father told Me. ¹⁶ You didn't choose Me. I chose you. I appointed you to go and produce lasting fruit, so that the Father will give you whatever you ask for, using My Name. ¹⁷ This is my command: Love each other. John 15:1-17 (NLT).

The resurrection of Jesus Christ from the dead began His spiritual union with His disciples, which is equivalent to the union He enjoys with God the Father (see John 15:4-5; 1 John 1:3). Jesus Christ lives (remains) in believers and believers also live in Jesus Christ through the Holy Spirit. The Holy Spirit is present with believers because of faith (trust and belief) in the message, work and life about Jesus Christ. Remaining or abiding in Jesus Christ means placing our total trust, faith and belief in Him as our Lord and Savior and obedience to His commands (see also 1 John 3:23-24; 1 John 4:15). To sustain a true spiritual life in the world, believers must remain intimately close to God the Father and Jesus Christ. As a result of this attachment to Jesus Christ, believers are transformed into the likeness of Jesus Christ and bear spiritual fruit (see John 13:34-35; John 14:15; John 15:9-10; 1 John 2:5; 1 John 5:2-3).

Abiding in Jesus Christ and letting the Holy Spirit guide and direct one's life produces a life pleasing to God, which cannot be accomplished solely by human effort (John 15:1-8; Galatians 5:16-26). Only the Holy Spirit can produce in believers a life that pleases God and produces "the fruit of the Spirit". Nevertheless, Jesus Christ instructed believers that to keep the Holy Spirit they must remain or "abide" close to Him. He knew in order for believers to live a life that was guided by the Spirit, they must live an intimate and enduring relationship with Jesus Christ throughout their lives.

Obeying Christ's teachings constitutes one way in which we can abide or remain close to Him (John 8:31). Jesus Christ clearly stated they when we remain in Jesus Christ by obeying his teachings, God the Father and God the Son (Jesus Christ) will remain in us (see also 1 John 2:14-17). A connection to Jesus Christ produces spiritual life and fruit—clusters of grapes (John 15:5). A constant connection with Jesus Christ allows His life to flow fruitfully through His true disciples. Sadly, anyone that does not abide with Jesus Christ and remain intimately close to Him will be separated from the Grapevine and His sustaining life.

The perseverance of the works of God and the Second Coming

> ⁶ *God began doing a good work in you, and I am sure*
> *He will continue it until it is finished when Jesus*
> *Christ comes again. Philippians 1:6 (NCV).*

The Holy Spirit lives in believers to enable them to be more like Jesus Christ every day. Rest assured that when God starts a project, He completes it! God will help believers grow in grace and in the likeness of Jesus Christ until He has completed His work in our lives (see Romans 8:29; Romans 9:16; Ephesians 1:3-11; Ephesians 2:4-10; Ephesians 4:13, 15). Christian growth is a race or fight (1 Corinthians 9:24-27; 2 Timothy 4:7). Being born again takes a simple moment of faith in Jesus Christ, but becoming like Jesus Christ is a lifelong process! The life that begins with the Holy Spirit depends on the Holy Spirit for its continuance (Galatians 3:3). As Christ fulfilled His mission in the power of the Spirit (Hebrews 9:14), so the person "in Christ" can only live life as a Christian out of the same Spirit.

CHAPTER 13
The Holy Spirit and Evangelism

*⁸ But when the Holy Spirit comes to you, you will receive power.
You will be my witnesses—in Jerusalem, in all of Judea, in
Samaria, and in every part of the world. ⁹ After He [Jesus
Christ] said this, as they were watching, He was lifted up,
and a cloud hid Him from their sight. Acts 1:8-9 (NCV).*

Jesus Christ's ascension into heaven marks the outpouring of the Holy
Spirit to all His followers. His last recorded words on earth were to go and
proclaim the Gospel throughout the world. He wanted all nations and races,
and both men and women, to know of His life, message, and love to the ends
of the earth so they could find heart peace with God. These last words of
Jesus are called the Great Commission and are recorded in five passages in
the New Testament — Matthew 28:16-20, Mark 16:15-18, Luke 24:46-49,
John 20:21-23, Acts 1:8. First, Jesus Christ knew that His followers would
need the Holy Spirit to proclaim His Good News message.

*⁴⁶ And He said, "Yes, it was written long ago that the Messiah
would suffer and die and rise from the dead on the third
day. ⁴⁷ It was also written that this message would be
proclaimed in the authority of His Name to all the nations,
beginning in Jerusalem: 'There is forgiveness of sins for all
who repent.' ⁴⁸ You are witnesses of all these things. ⁴⁹ "And
now I will send the Holy Spirit, just as my Father promised.
But stay here in the city <u>until</u> the Holy Spirit comes and
fills you <u>with power</u> from heaven." Luke 24:46-49 (NLT).*

Jesus Christ specifically tells His disciples in Luke 24:46-49 they must wait for the Holy Spirit to arrive to strengthen and empower them to build the church and spread the Gospel (John 14:26; Acts 1:8). Notice the sequence or chain of Jesus Christ's commissioning to His disciples:

(1) The disciples would receive the Holy Spirit,
(2) He would give each disciple power, and
(3) The disciples would proclaim and witness the Good News of Jesus Christ with amazing results and power.

Jesus Christ understood that His disciples needed the Holy Spirit to carry out and obey His commission to take the Gospel to the world. The commission given by Jesus Christ is Holy Spirit-powered and Holy Spirit-guided. Jesus Christ knew that, to do God's work, His disciples needed the Holy Spirit and His spiritual gifts to fulfill the Great Commission.

> *21 So Jesus said to them again, "Peace to you! As the Father has sent Me, I also send you." 22 And when He had said this, He breathed on them, and said to them, "Receive the Holy Spirit. 23 If you forgive the sins of any, they are forgiven them; if you retain the sins of any, they are retained." John 20:21-23 (NKJV).*

In John 20:21-23, the Holy Scriptures record the first giving of the Holy Spirit to the disciples by Jesus Christ to obey the Great Commission. Here, Jesus Christ breathes the Holy Spirit onto his disciples. However, at Pentecost (Acts 2:1-4) a more dramatic and heavy outpouring of the Holy Spirit to all people present occurs for all those who placed their faith and trust in Jesus Christ as Lord and Savior. Before then, the Holy Spirit had not been poured out generously to all people. At the Day of Pentecost, Jesus Christ poured the Holy Spirit on His followers and fulfilled His promise that the Spirit would be given to all people equally who call faithfully on the Name of the Lord in faith (Joel 2:32; John 14:15-26; John 15:26; and John 16:7-15).

> *6 So He [God] said to me [Prophet Zechariah], "This is the word of the Lord to Zerubbabel: 'Not by might nor by power, but by My Spirit,' says the Lord Almighty." Zechariah 4:6 (NIV).*

The Holy Spirit's outpouring at Pentecost significantly influenced the spread of the Gospel message of Jesus Christ in the Book of Acts and throughout the New Testament. With the Holy Spirit, disciples of Jesus Christ were empowered to take the Good News of Jesus Christ to the ends of the earth (Acts 1:8; Acts 2:4-18). Disciples such as Stephen and Philip were filled with the Holy Spirit and preached by His power and presence (Acts 6 – 8). Moreover, the Apostle Paul's ministry was charged with the Holy Spirit's energy from the beginning (Acts 9:17).

Throughout the Book of Acts and even to our present generation, the disciples of Jesus Christ accomplish its missionary outreach and evangelism through the power, guidance, and direction of the Holy Spirit. The Holy Spirit empowers and guides followers of Jesus Christ to obey the Great Commission and tell the wonderful Good News of Jesus Christ to others (Matthew 28:18-20; Acts 11:12; 13:2; 15:28; 16:6-7; 20:22; 21:11). Throughout the New Testament and up through present times, there have been numerous instances where the Good News massage has been proclaimed even in the face of active resistance and hostility; the Holy Spirit overcomes all obstacles so the Good News massage can continue throughout the world. The Holy Spirit convinces and convicts people to obey and follow Jesus Christ, in the same way that the disciples carry out the Great Commission.

Remember, obedience to God's will (and the carrying out of his Good News message) is not meant to be carried out merely under the disciples' own strength. Jesus Christ never expected His disciples to do it on their own. Instead, Jesus Christ instructed His disciples then and today to rely on the power of the Holy Spirit to obey and carry out the Great Commission (Luke 24:49; Acts 1:8; Acts 2:4, 17-18). God's Holy Spirit living on the inside strengthens disciples of Jesus Christ to tell the Good News message successfully around the world. The Holy Spirit gives each disciple power to witness for Jesus Christ beyond his or her everyday abilities. This power from the Holy Spirit includes confidence, courage, boldness, insight, and authority. Disciples of Jesus Christ need all these gifts to fulfill the Great Commission and spread the Good News of Jesus Christ.

As the disciples obey Jesus Christ's Great Commission, they have comfort in the knowledge that He is always with them through the Holy Spirit's Presence. As the Gospel of Matthew states, Jesus Christ is our Immanuel, "God is with us" (Matthew 1:23).

CHAPTER 14
Overcoming Life's Struggles

⁷ Then you will experience God's peace, which exceeds anything we can understand. His peace will guard your hearts and minds as you live in Christ Jesus. Philippians 4:7 (NLT).

²⁷ Peace I leave with you; My peace I give you. I do not give to you as the world gives. Do not let your hearts be troubled and do not be afraid. John 14:27 (NIV).

Believers have always had to face hardships and struggles in many forms: persecution, sickness, harassment, imprisonment, even death. These difficulties could cause people to fear that God has abandoned them. But when a person accepts God through Jesus Christ as Lord and Savior, he or she gains all the privileges and responsibilities of a child in God's family. One of the great privileges of being in God's family is the presence of the Holy Spirit from within our hearts (see Romans 8:16; Galatians 4:5-6). God's Holy Spirit brings peace and comfort as our spirits cry out to the Holy Spirit with any pain or circumstance. Unlike worldly peace, God's peace from the Holy Spirit guarantees believers that in any circumstance He will never leave, forsake, or abandon us. Nothing can separate Jesus Christ's faithful presence from His believers (Matthew 28:20; Romans 8:35-39).

¹⁶ And I will pray to the Father, and He will give you another Helper, that He may abide with you forever ¹⁷ the Spirit of Truth, whom the world cannot receive, because it neither sees Him nor knows Him; but you know Him, for

*He dwells with you and will be in you. ¹⁸ I will not leave
you orphans; I will come to you. John 14:16-18 (NKJV).*

Jesus Christ sent the Holy Spirit to believers as a gift to live *with* and *within*
all true believers (John 14:17). The Holy Spirit is God working with, around,
and inside believers every day. To have the Holy Spirit is to have Jesus Christ
Himself (John 14:18), who never leaves or abandons us (John 14:16). In
difficult times, the Holy Spirit is present as our Helper, Advocate, and Strength
to overcome stressful circumstances and situations (see John 14:27). The Holy
Spirit brings inner peace to our hearts, bodies, and minds (see John 14:27).
The Holy Spirit who comes to live in believers is the Spirit of Christ Himself,
which provides our peace, assurance, and God's presence.

*²⁶ Also, the Spirit helps us with our weakness. We do not know
how to pray as we should. But the Spirit Himself speaks to God
for us, even begs God for us with deep feelings that words cannot
explain. ²⁷ God can see what is in people's hearts. And He knows
what is in the mind of the Spirit, because the Spirit speaks to God
for His people in the way God wants. Romans 8:26-27 (NCV).*

*¹⁸ Now all of us can come to the Father through the same Holy Spirit
because of what Christ has done for us. Ephesians 2:18 (NLT).*

Also, the Holy Spirit works to provide all people — Jews and Gentiles (non-
Jews) — full access to God the Father in prayer in difficult circumstances
(Ephesians 2:18). Because of Jesus Christ's sacrifice for sins on the Cross at
Calvary, believers receive the Holy Spirit to approach God openly through
prayer (see Ephesians 3:12; Acts 10:34-37, 44-48; 1 Peter 3:18). In the prayer
life of believers, the Holy Spirit intercedes and prays for us before God. Even
more, the Holy Spirit empowers believers' prayers and makes them effective.
One specific kind of prayer that the New Testament says is empowered by
the Holy Spirit is the gift of prayer in tongues (see 1 Corinthians 12:10-11; 1
Corinthians 14:2; 14-17).

*¹⁷ Put on salvation as your helmet, and take the sword of the
Spirit, which is the Word of God. Ephesians 6:17 (NLT).*

Another work of the Holy Spirit is empowering believers to overcome
any spiritual hostility, attacks or opposition. Simply put, the Holy Spirit
strengthens believers for spiritual warfare that opposes them. Fear, sin, evil,
uncertainty, doubt, and numerous other forces are all at war within and
around believers. However, the Holy Spirit is the peace within our hearts

and lives to restrain these hostile forces against us. The Holy Spirit uses the Word of God to distinguish between spirits and defeat evil. The Word of God functions as the "sword of the Spirit".[4]

> *[12] For the Word of God is alive and powerful. It is sharper than the sharpest two-edged sword, cutting between soul and spirit, between joint and marrow. It exposes our innermost thoughts and desires. Hebrews 4:12 (NLT).*

The sword of the Spirit is the only weapon of offense against evil attacks, hostility, and opposition. When believers are tempted, we need to trust in the truth of God's Word. Sadly, all believers are sometimes engaged in a spiritual battle and find themselves subject to evil's attacks because they are no longer on evil's side. To withstand evil attacks and hostility, believers must depend on God's Holy Spirit and His Word and fight evil using the strength of the Holy Spirit's power living within us.

The Book of Acts highlights the presence and power of the Holy Spirit in the early Christians and their many struggles. Because of the status of the Holy Spirit's work in Acts, the Book has often been called "the Acts of the Holy Spirit." Early church believers in the Book of Acts overcame many obstacles to spread the Good News of Jesus Christ. For instance, Stephen and Philip were filled with the Holy Spirit and preached by His power and direction despite hostile opposition (Acts 6–8). Moreover, the Apostle Paul's ministry was empowered and strengthen with a strong presence of the Holy Spirit as his guide and energy after encounter with Jesus Christ (Acts 9:17; Acts 13:4).

> *[11] Whenever you are arrested and brought to trial, do not worry beforehand about what to say. Just say whatever is given you at the time, for it is not you speaking, but the Holy Spirit. Mark 13:11 (NIV).*

> *[13] If you then, though you are evil, know how to give good gifts to your children, how much more will your Father in heaven give the Holy Spirit to those who ask him! Luke 11:13 (NIV).*

Jesus Christ promised the help of the Holy Spirit in times of trial (Mark 13:11). The Holy Spirit gives believers courage and the right words to say in time of trouble (see also Matthew 5:11). Jesus Christ sends His Spirit to strengthen believers who are persecuted. To receive boldness, believers only

---

4   That is why believers MUST read and study the Holy Bible.

needs to pray for the power of the Holy Spirit to give them courage, strength, and confidence (Luke 11:13). The Holy Spirit helps believers in their weakness (Romans 8:26).

God has given believers the Holy Spirit to fill our hearts with His love and peace (see Jeremiah 31:33-34; Acts 2:17-21; Romans 5:5). Only when God's Holy Spirit is present within a person's heart can one achieve true peace and fruitfulness (Ezekiel 36:22-38; Galatians 5:22-23). God's Holy Word promises that world peace will happen in the end times. The outpouring of world peace described in Isaiah 32 will occur worldwide when God's Kingdom is established for all eternity (see Joel 2:28-29). Nevertheless, believers can also experience God's peace now through His Holy Spirit's presence from within us. God's peace is available to all believers through Jesus Christ.

Sometimes, God uses persecution and struggle to spread the Good News of Jesus Christ's love. Through persecution and struggle, believers in the Book of Acts fled Jerusalem. Persecution forced the first century believers after into Judea, Samaria, and throughout the world — thus fulfilling the Great Commission (See Acts 1:8).

> [26] *In the same way the Spirit also helps our weakness; for we do not know how to pray as we should, but the Spirit Himself intercedes for us with groanings too deep for words;* [27] *and He who searches the hearts knows what the mind of the Spirit is, because He intercedes for the saints according to the will of God. Romans 8:26-27 (NASB).*

As a believer of Jesus Christ, you are not left alone here on earth to handle and cope with life's problems. Even when you do not know the right words to pray, the Holy Spirit prays on our behalf before God, and God answers. With God's Spirit helping us pray, a believer should never be afraid to come before God the Father. Always pray and ask the Holy Spirit to intercede and pray for you "in accordance with God's will." Then, when you bring your prayers and requests to God, trust that God will always do what is best.

During our struggles, the Holy Spirit brings an atmosphere of peace into situations. The Holy Spirit imparts an atmosphere of joy (see also Acts 13:51; 1 Thessalonians 1:6). God is "not a God of confusion but of peace" (1 Corinthians 14:33 - NKJV). In spite of the circumstances and struggles believers face, they are not alone. God's Holy Spirit is present. Believers can rest in the peace of Jesus Christ's Holy Spirit in the most troublesome times.

*²⁰ Teach these new disciples to obey all the commands
I have given you. And be sure of this: I [Jesus Christ]
am with you always, even to the end of the age."
Matthew 28:20 (NLT).*

*²⁷ "I am leaving you with a gift — peace of mind and
heart. And the peace I give is a gift the world cannot
give. So don't be troubled or afraid. John 14:27 (NLT).*

*⁶ And now just as you trusted Christ to save you, trust Him, too,
for each day's problems; live in vital union with Him. ⁷ Let your
roots grow down into Him and draw up nourishment from Him.
See that you go on growing in the Lord, and become strong and
vigorous in the truth you were taught. Let your lives overflow with
joy and thanksgiving for all He has done. Colossians 2:6-7 (TLB).*

CHAPTER 15
The Holy Spirit and the Power of God

> *¹⁹ I also pray that you will understand the incredible greatness of God's power for us who believe Him. This is the same mighty power ²⁰ that raised Christ from the dead and seated Him in the place of honor at God's right hand in the heavenly realms. Ephesians 1:19-20 (NLT).*

The Holy Spirit is the power of God. One of the works of the Holy Spirit is to reveal the active power of God to the world, especially to the body of Jesus Christ (the Church). Through faith in Jesus Christ, anyone can freely receive God's empowering Holy Spirit and have all the fullness of God readily available to walk with and within daily (Colossians 2:9-10; 1 John 3:24). Having the Holy Spirit's power make His home within believers' hearts through faith is the source of all spiritual power (see John 14:16-17, 23; John 15:4-5; Galatians 2:20).

> *² Let me ask you this one question: Did you receive the Holy Spirit by trying to keep the Jewish laws? Of course not, for the Holy Spirit came upon you only after you heard about Christ and trusted [believed or had faith in] Him to save you... ⁵ I ask you again, does God give you the power of the Holy Spirit and work miracles among you as a result of your trying to obey the Jewish laws? No, of course not. It is when you believe [trust or had faith] in Christ and fully trust Him. Galatians 3:2, 5 (TLB).*

In the present New Testament era, people cannot receive the Holy Spirit's power by obeying the law of Moses nor by following any special rules or rituals. As has also been talked about through this book, one cannot receive the Holy Spirit's power merely by human effort (flesh). Instead, people can <u>only</u> receive the Holy Spirit's power and grow spiritually by turning from their sins and turning to God through faith in Jesus Christ. Once a person trusts Jesus Christ, they began their Christian lives in the power of the Holy Spirit and continue to grow in their Christian faith by continually walking in the Holy Spirit's power. Through prayer and faith, a believer can ask and receive the Holy Spirit's power to fill every aspect of one's life to the fullest and live righteous lives for Jesus Christ. This power helps believers in life and in ministry (John 14 — 16).

No one, despite their best human efforts, can earn his or her way to God and receive His Holy Spirit's power by keeping a set of rules or rituals such as obeying the Ten Commandments, attending church faithfully, or doing good deeds. Such efforts in the absence of turning to God through faith in Jesus Christ only lead to frustration and heartache. While certain disciplines (such as Bible study and prayer and service to others) may help us grow these actions must not take the place of the Holy Spirit in us. Believers become more and more like Jesus Christ with His power as we live with Him day by day through faith in the Holy Spirit. Turn your eyes and heart in faith daily to Jesus Christ and away from your own performance. This is the only way to live and receive the Holy Spirit's power to joyous living.

> *¹ So there is now no condemnation awaiting*
> *those who belong to Christ Jesus.*
> *² For the power of the life-giving Spirit — and this*
> *power is mine through Christ Jesus — has freed*
> *me from the vicious circle of sin and death.*
> *Romans 8:1-2 (TLB).*

> *⁹ But you are not ruled by your sinful selves. You are*
> *ruled by the Spirit, if that Spirit of God really lives in*
> *you. But the person who does not have the Spirit of*
> *Christ does not belong to Christ. Romans 8:9 (NCV).*

> *¹⁰ Create in me a pure heart, God, and make my spirit*
> *right again. ¹¹ Do not send me away from you or take your*
> *Holy Spirit away from me. ¹² Give me back the joy of your*
> *salvation. Keep me strong by giving me a willing spirit.*
> *Psalms 51:10-12 (NCV).*

Only the power of the Holy Spirit can change a person's heart and make it holy, pure, and willing to obey God (Psalm 51:10, 12). Sadly, because all humans are born sinners (Genesis 3; Psalm 51:5), our natural tendency is to sin and please ourselves rather than please God. Moreover, non-believers of Jesus Christ continue to be controlled and led by sin and fleshly desires derived from Adam and Eve (Genesis 3). Like David, we must pray and ask God's Holy Spirit to cleanse our hearts and spirits from sin and evil from within and instead create a pure heart and spirit with new thoughts and desires (Psalm 51:7). Through faith, the Holy Spirit gives believers great power to live for God and not sin. The Holy Spirit provides the gift of persistence, guidance, and freedom. Often the Holy Spirit's best work is teaching us to persist, to keep on doing what is right and living a Christ-like life. The Holy Spirit does not eliminate human ideas or thoughts, or make it impossible for believers to sin. However, the Holy Spirit is the most powerful force in believers' lives and helps providers flee from and resist the continuing power of sin. The Holy Spirit opposes sin in a believer's life and brings holiness and righteousness.

> *⁶ Then he told me, "This is the word of the Lord to Zerubbabel: 'You will not succeed by your own strength or power, but by My Spirit,' says the Lord All-Powerful. Zechariah 4:6 (NCV).*

> *⁵ For we know how dearly God loves us, because He has given us the Holy Spirit to fill our hearts with His love. Romans 5:5 (NLT).*

> *¹⁸ Be filled instead with the Holy Spirit and controlled by Him. Ephesians 5:18 (TLB).*

Believers must depend on the Holy Spirit's power for everyday living because the Holy Spirit is the power of God working for us (Zechariah 4:6). God the Father and His Son Jesus Christ sent God the Holy Spirit to fill believers' lives with love and to enable them to live by His power (Acts 1:8; Romans 5:5). Through His power, the Holy Spirit works in the hearts of believers to live fruitful, Christ-like lives (Galatians 5:22-23). The Holy Spirit provides believers with power to overcome sin and evil in their lives (Ephesians 5:18). Even through believers may continue to experience the desire to sin in their lives, they can please God and overcome sin by yielding to the Holy Spirit's guidance (Galatians 5:16-18).

> *¹⁴ And God is going to raise our bodies from the dead by His power just as He raised up the Lord Jesus Christ. 1 Corinthians 6:14 (TLB).*

> *¹⁸ Christ suffered for our sins once for all time. He never*

sinned, but He died for sinners to bring you safely home to God. He suffered physical death, but He was raised to life in the Spirit. 1 Peter 3:18 (NLT).

The Holy Spirit brings life giving power. He is the Agent of new life, renewal, and resurrection (Isaiah 32:15-20). Most important, the Holy Spirit was the life-giving power that raised Jesus Christ from the dead (1 Corinthians 6:14). The power of God that brought Jesus Christ's body back from the dead is available to believers to bring our morally and spiritually dead selves back to life (1Corinthians 15:12-19). The Holy Spirit guarantees our physical bodies will be raised to newness of life (Ephesians 1:13-14) because He is God's promise of eternal life with Jesus Christ forever for those who believe in God through faith in Jesus Christ (see Romans 8:23; 1 Corinthians 6:14; 2 Corinthians 4:14; 1 Thessalonians 4:14).

[4] He [Jesus Christ] was shown to be the Son of God when He was raised from the dead by the power of the Holy Spirit. He is Jesus Christ our Lord. Romans 1:4 (NLT).

[10] And Christ lives within you, so even though your body will die because of sin, the Spirit gives you life because you have been made right with God. [11] The Spirit of God, who raised Jesus from the dead, lives in you. And just as God raised Christ Jesus from the dead, He will give life to your mortal bodies by this same Spirit living within you. Romans 8:10-11 (NLT).

Jesus Christ suffered actual physical death (literally death in the flesh) on the Cross at Calvary. However, the power of the Holy Spirit raised Jesus Christ from the dead and gave Him life. Through this same Spirit, Jesus Christ's lives in all believers through faith in His message, life, death, and resurrection. The mighty power at work within believers is the same power of the living God that raised Jesus Christ from the dead (see Ephesians 1:19-20). By that same power, God is able to accomplish infinitely more than we might ask or think, because God is at work in the lives of His children.

[14] When I think of all this, I fall to my knees and pray to the Father, [15] the Creator of everything in heaven and on earth. [16] I pray that from His glorious, unlimited resources He will empower you with inner strength through His Spirit. [17] Then Christ will make His home in your hearts as you trust in Him. Your roots will grow down into God's love and keep you strong. [18] And may you have the power to understand, as all God's people should, how wide, how long, how high, and how deep His love is. [19]

May you experience the love of Christ, though it is too great to understand fully. Then you will be made complete with all the fullness of life and power that comes from God. [20] Now all glory to God, who is able, through His mighty power at work within us, to accomplish infinitely more than we might ask or think. [21] Glory to Him in the church and in Christ Jesus through all generations forever and ever! Amen. Ephesians 3:14-21 (NLT).

Conclusion

Who is the Holy Spirit? The Holy Spirit is God and the active presence of God on earth. He moved over the face of the waters in Genesis, came upon Moses in the wilderness, inspired the prophets and the apostles, rose Jesus Christ from death just to name a few of His mighty works. The Holy Spirit is the greatest gift God gives people through faith in Jesus Christ. The Holy Spirit is the Spirit of God and Jesus Christ living inside of believers—God's Presence.

The Holy Spirit is a part of the Trinity —God the Father, God the Son (Jesus Christ), and God the Holy Spirit. When a person sincerely trusts Jesus Christ for salvation, the Holy Spirit comes to live inside of him or her and fills that person's innermost being. The Holy Spirit transforms people from within to become more Christ-like. A believer's moral conduct and love for God and others proves God's presence in our lives. The Holy Spirit brings about Christ-like behavior and obedience to God (Galatians 5:22-23). The Holy Spirit living inside believers brings empowerment, direction, and strength to live and serve others according to the teachings and commands of the Holy Bible. Most importantly, the Holy Spirit transforms believers so they are able to live, act, and look more like Jesus Christ and want to become part of God's plan to build up His church. Simply put, the Holy Spirit within believers helps us please God every day.

Moreover, the Holy Spirit is the presence of God at work in the world. Because the Holy Spirit's presence, people are made aware of sin and their need for God. Many people are unaware of the Holy Spirit's presence and activities. However, to believers who receive and love God through Jesus Christ, the Holy Spirit gives a whole new way to look at life. The Holy Spirit provides an overwhelming heart peace with God and comfort through prayer.

Unlike worldly peace, which is usually defined as the absence of conflict, this peace is confident assurance in any circumstance God is present!

By faith, believers of Jesus Christ can call upon the Holy Spirit's power each day for daily use and help in any of life's situation. The Holy Spirit directs a believer's heart, path and helps a believer choose right from wrong. Also, the Holy Spirit counsels, helps, encourages, and strengthens a believer of Jesus Christ. As the Spirit of Truth, the Holy Spirit teaches believers the truths of Jesus Christ.

When Jesus Christ ascended into heaven, His physical presence left the earth. The God through Jesus Christ promised to send the Holy Spirit as our Comforter and Advocate to care for, guide, and help His disciples and also to provide instruction, sanctification, and guidance. Jesus Christ kept His promise at Pentecost that continues today. This same God through Jesus— who lived with the disciples, who died and was buried, and who rose from the dead—now lives on the in the hearts of believers to love and be with them always. As promised during His earthly ministry, God through Jesus Christ poured out the Holy Spirit so that His spiritual presence would still be among His people.

During the Old Testament period, the empowering gift of God's Holy Spirit had previously been given only to select individuals such as Judges, priests, kings, and prophets. With the New Covenant today, the Holy Spirit now comes to live in ALL people, regardless of race, gender, or status, who have sincerely trusted Jesus Christ for their salvation and acknowledged Him as Lord and Savior. In essence, you can receive the Holy Spirit simply through heart faith in Jesus Christ and through asking in prayer for His presence to come live in your heart.

The Holy Spirit begins the Christian experience with God through Jesus Christ. No believer can be united with Jesus Christ, adopted as God's children, nor become a part of the body of Christ except by baptism in the Holy Spirit. The Holy Spirit is the power of believers' lives. He begins the lifetime process of changing believers to become more like Jesus Christ. The Holy Spirit works in believers to help us become like Jesus Christ. When we receive Jesus Christ by faith as Lord and Savior, believers begin a personal and intimate relationship with God through Jesus Christ. Moreover, the Holy Spirit unifies the Christian community in Jesus Christ and He can be experienced by all. He works through all people through faith.

Many people think of the Holy Spirit as being an experience of divine power. The Holy Spirit in both the Old Testament and the New Testament is the core of the experience of new life, strength, and energy and liberation from sin and death. As God, the Holy Spirit brings spiritual refreshment and renewal. The Holy Spirit is the power of God that transforms the individual into the image of God and makes the believer like Jesus Christ. The Holy Spirit is the agent of holiness for the church and its leaders. He keeps the church pure and He promotes holiness in its members.

The Prophet Zechariah calls the Spirit "a spirit of grace and prayer" (Zechariah 12:10-12). In the same way, the Holy Spirit helps believers in our weakness. Often, we do not know what we to pray for, but the Holy Spirit Himself intercedes for us with groans that words cannot express. All of these benefits of the Holy Spirit are available by simply asking God to fill you with the Holy Spirit once you accept Jesus Christ as Lord and Savior.

No matter how impure your life is right now, God offers everyone a fresh start through faith in Jesus Christ. Through heart faith in God through Jesus Christ, a person can have his or her sins washed away and receive a new heart and spirit from God. The Holy Spirit has the power to make new people and creates a new life.

The Holy Spirit's presence is in believers' lives, not only spiritual and mystical. The Holy Spirit is a powerful Person on our side, working for and around us. He teaches, helps, and guides believers toward all truth. Moreover, the Holy Spirit ministers to both the head and the heart and gives us the power, strength, and ability genuinely to love and to overcome hatred and evil in our world. A believer does not have to wait for a certain feeling or emotion to know that the Holy Spirit has come within. You will know the Holy Spirit has come because Jesus Christ promised He would in John 14 - 16.

A believer's complete focus and hope must be on trusting God, relying on His Holy Spirit, and loving others. In essence, if people live their lives guided and directed by the Holy Spirit, loving God and others, they are in perfect harmony and obedience with the intent of God's Law. People who produce and reveal the fruit of the Spirit satisfy the Law of God. At the right time, believers will reap a blessing from God walking in step with the Holy Spirit.

So, yield your life fully to God. Ask God for His Holy Spirit in every area and circumstance of life. Then, live and pray each day by the Holy Spirit.

> [20] *But you, dear friends, carefully build yourselves up in this most holy faith by praying in the Holy Spirit. Jude 1:20 (MSG).*

¹³ If you then, though you are evil, know how to give good gifts to your children, how much more will your Father in heaven give the Holy Spirit to those who ask him! Luke 11:13 (NIV).

PRAY TO GOD TO SEND THE HOLY SPIRIT!

Salvation Call

16 For God so loved the world that He gave His only begotten Son, that whoever believes in Him should not perish but have everlasting life. 17 For God did not send His Son into the world to condemn the world, but that the world through Him might be saved. — John 3:16-17 (NKJV).

GOD LOVES YOU AND HE CARES ABOUT ALL YOUR NEEDS. God loved you so much that He became a Man through Jesus Christ. Jesus Christ is God's only Son. God gave His only Son Jesus Christ to die for the sins of the entire world on the Cross at Calvary on a Friday afternoon more than 2000 years ago. Three days later on Sunday morning, God raised Jesus Christ from the dead to offer salvation to all people.

Salvation is God's gift to all people. No one can earn salvation by work or effort, but only through faith in Jesus Christ (Ephesians 2:1-10). By having faith and belief in Jesus Christ's sacrificial death on the Cross for your sins, you are made right with God the Father and declared holy and righteous (Romans 3:21-31). Most importantly, you will now have a personal relationship with God through Jesus Christ. You can approach God about all your concerns and needs through prayer.

Now, this belief in Jesus Christ is more than an intellectual agreement that Jesus is God. This belief means placing your complete trust, hope, and confidence in Jesus Christ's life, death, and resurrection as payment for your sins and acceptance of Him as Lord over your complete life. While our good works and efforts do not save us, God saves us so we can *do* good works of love for others.

After rising from the dead, Jesus Christ ascended into heaven and His physical presence left the earth (Acts 1:1-11). Nevertheless, Jesus Christ sent the Holy

Spirit so that His Spiritual Presence would still be among all humanity who had faith in His life, death, and resurrection.

Our next step is faith in Jesus Christ. The Holy Bible tells us that everyone has fallen short and sinned against God, even with our so-called good and nice deeds (Romans 3:23). The wages of sin against God are death, darkness, and despair (Romans 6:23). Yet the GOOD NEWS is that God has sent His special gift, His Son Jesus Christ, to suffer for our sins. You can receive this gift from God simply by calling on the name of Jesus Christ, to accept Jesus with all your heart as your Lord and Savior, ask Him to cleanse you from all your sins, and then you are SAVED! (Romans 10:13). With that simple prayer, you have become a new creature in Jesus Christ (2 Corinthians 5:17).

Find a good Holy Bible to read daily. The Holy Bible is God's love letter to you. Then, find a good Bible-believing church to serve and worship God. Church is a good way to find other believers in Jesus Christ who can help you daily in your love walk.

CONGRATULATIONS!

ABOUT THE AUTHOR

Lola Richey is a native and lifelong resident of South Carolina and a believer in Jesus Christ. She is a graduate of Winthrop University in Rock Hill, South Carolina, with a Bachelor of Science in Business Administration, with an Accounting Concentration. Ms. Richey obtained her law degree from the University of South Carolina School of Law (Juris Doctorate) and Masters of Taxation (LL.M.) from the University of Florida College of Law. A Certified Public Accountant (CPA) licensed in the State of Maryland, Ms. Richey has studied at Erskine Theological Seminary in Due West, South Carolina. She is a Gulf War Veteran serving as a Hospital Corpsman and as a United States Naval Officer (Supply Corp).

She is married to Rodney W. Richey and has two sons, Jonathan and Joseph.

NOTE TO THE READER

The publisher invites all to share their comments, responses, and suggestions about this book by writing to:

Network of Glory, Inc.
102 Red Branch Lane
Simpsonville, South Carolina 29681

Thank you for reading and GOD BLESS!

Further Scripture References
For Growth And Leadership

Old Testament

Genesis 1:1-3
Genesis 41:37-40
Exodus 3:13-14
Exodus 7:3-4
Exodus 31:1-6
Exodus 33:11
Exodus 34:6-7
Exodus 34:28
Leviticus 8:35
Leviticus 10:3
Leviticus 11:44-45
Leviticus 19:2
Numbers 11:16-17
Numbers 11:24-30
Numbers 16:1-50
Numbers 24:2
Deuteronomy 7:19
Deuteronomy 13:1-18
Joshua 7:11-12
Judges 3:9-11
Judges 6:34
Judges 9:23
Judges 11:29
Judges 14:5-6
Judges 16:20-21
1 Samuel 2:1-2
1 Samuel 2:25
1 Samuel 10:1-10

Jeremiah 23:29
Jeremiah 31:33-34
Ezekiel 1:24
Ezekiel 8:1-18
Ezekiel 11:5
Ezekiel 11:19-20
Ezekiel 15:1-5
Ezekiel 16:9
Ezekiel 16:61-63
Ezekiel 18:30-32
Ezekiel 34:23-25
Ezekiel 36:26-27
Ezekiel 37:1-28
Ezekiel 39:29
Daniel 1:21
Daniel 2:49
Hosea 8:7
Hosea 10:1-2
Hosea 11:9
Joel 2:28-32
Haggai 2:5
Zechariah 12:10-14

New Testament

Matthew 3:11
Matthew 5:9
Matthew 5:43-48
Matthew 22:31-32
Matthew 24:10-13
Matthew 28:19
Mark 3:28-29
Mark 8:11-13
Luke 1:15
Luke 1:35
Luke 1:41
Luke 1:67
Luke 2:24-27
Luke 3:22
Luke 4:1
Luke 4:18

Luke 6:35-36
Luke 15:31
Luke 19:21-23
Luke 22:28
Luke 24:49
John 3:1-15, 36
John 6:56-57
John 7:37
John 8:31
John 14
John 15
John 16
John 20:22-23
Acts 1:4-8, 16
Acts 2
Acts 4:8
Acts 4:31
Acts 5:32
Acts 6:1-7
Acts 7:55
Acts 8:15
Acts 8:17
Acts 8:29, 39
Acts 9:3
Acts 9:15-17, 21
Acts 9:31
Acts 10:19-20
Acts 10:44-48
Acts 11:12
Acts 11:24
Acts 13:1-9
Acts 13:52
Acts 14:3
Acts 15:28
Acts 16:6
Acts 17:16-17
Acts 19:6-7
Acts 20:28
Acts 22:16
Acts 24:25
Romans 1:1-4

Ephesians 1:9-14
Ephesians 1:19-23
Ephesians 2:1-8
Ephesians 2:14-3:13
Ephesians 4:2-8
Ephesians 4:11-16
Ephesians 4:17-5:20
Ephesians 5:23-29
Ephesians 6:11-18
Philippians 3:12-13, 21
Philippians 4:1, 6-7
Colossians 1:12-27
Colossians 2:12, 20-23
Colossians 3:1-15
1 Thessalonians 1:5-6
1 Thessalonians 4:3-7
1 Thessalonians 5:19-20
2 Thessalonians 1:11
2 Thessalonians 2:2, 8
2 Thessalonians 2:13-15
2 Thessalonians 3:3
1 Timothy 1:16
1 Timothy 2:5
1 Timothy 3:15
2 Timothy 1:6
2 Timothy 3:1-9
2 Timothy 3:16-17
2 Timothy 4:2
Titus 1:8
Titus 3:4-7
Hebrews 1:3
Hebrews 2:1-4
Hebrews 3:7-11
Hebrews 3:15
Hebrews 4:12
Hebrews 6:4-8
Hebrews 8:6
Hebrews 9:8, 15
Hebrews 10:15-17, 22
Hebrews 10:26-31
Hebrews 12:1-29

Hebrews 13:17
James 1:21
James 5:10-11
1 Peter 2:1
1 Peter 1:11-18
1 Peter 2:5-10, 16
1 Peter 4:10-14
2 Peter 1:9
2 Peter 1:20-21
2 Peter 2:1-22
2 Peter 3:15
1 John 1:9
1 John 2:1
1 John 2:18-20
1 John 2:27-28
1 John 3:2
1 John 3:24
1 John 4:1-3
1 John 4:13
1 John 5:6
Jude 20-21
Revelation 1:4-5
Revelation 1:15
Revelation 2:10
Revelation 11:11
Revelation 13:10
Revelation 19:6-8
Revelation 21:5-8
Revelation 22:12-16

Related References

Packer, J.I. *Concise Theology: A Guide to Historic Christian Beliefs*. Tyndale House Publishers. 1993.

Draper, Charles. *Holman Illustrated Bible Dictionary*. Holman Reference. 2003.

Life Application Study Bible. Tyndale House Publishers. 2005.

NIV Study Bible. Zondervan, 2008.

Douglas, J.D. and Merrill C. Tenney. *NIV Compact Dictionary of the Bible*. Zondervan. 1989.

NLT Study Bible. Tyndale House Publishers. 2008.

Thompson Chain Reference Bible (NASB). Kirkbride Bible Company. 1996.